PABLO PICASSO
ANDRÉ SALMON

and

"Young French Painting"

by

JACQUELINE GOJARD

With Salmon's *Young French Painting*

TRANSLATED AND ANNOTATED BY

Beth S. Gersh-Nešić and Jacqueline Gojard

Copyright © 2022
Jacqueline Gojard and Beth S. Gersh-Nešić
All rights reserved (Tous droits réservés)

ISBN-13: 978-1-950191-02-4

Library of Congress Control Number: 2021930617

Cover design: Ruby Silvious **www.rubysilvious.com**
Interior design: Najdan Mancic **www.iskonbookdesign.com**

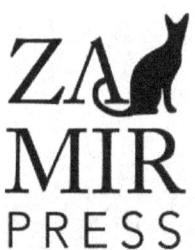

A division of

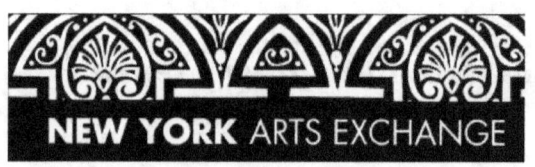

www.nyarts-exchange.com

DEDICATION

Nous tenons à saluer la mémoire de Léo Salmon et à remercier nos époux Jacques et Dušan qui nous ont aidées et soutenues dans ce minutieux travail de réédition.

We dedicate this book to the memory of Madame Léo Salmon, André Salmon's widow, and we thank our husbands Jacques and Dušan for their help and support as we endeavored with great care to complete this publication.

—BGN and JG

Contents

LIST OF ILLUSTRATIONS

Figure 1. Cover of *La Jeune Peinture française*, Paris: Société des Trente, Albert Messein, 1912.

Figure 2. Henri Adolphe Laissement (1854-1921), *Salon of French Artists in 1911*, 1911-12, oil on canvas, 125 x 178.5 cm (49 $\frac{3}{16}$ x 70 ¼ in.). Private Collection, Public Domain.

Figure 3. Odilon Redon, *Vase of Flowers*, 1900-1910, Pastel on board, 46.2 x 38.7 cm (18 $\frac{3}{16}$ x 15 ¼ in.), Gift of Edward R. Schaible, Class of 1934, Princeton University Art Museum. Wikipedia: Public Domain.

Figure 4. Albert Marquet, *Matisse in Manguin's Studio*, 1905, oil on board, 100 x 73 cm (39 ¼ x 28 ⅞ in.) Musée National d'Art Moderne, Centre Georges Pompidou, Paris, Wikipedia: Public Domain.

Figure 5. Henri Rousseau, *The Dream*, 1910, oil on canvas, 204.5 x 298.5 cm (6' 8 ½ x 9' 9 ½ in.) Museum of Modern Art, New York, Wikipedia: Public Domain.

Figure 6. Fauves Exhibition at the Salon d'Automne, in *L'Illustration*, November 4, 1905.

Figure 7. Othon Friesz, *The Bathers of Andelys*, 1908, oil on canvas, 97 x 162 cm (38 ⅛ inches x 63 ⅞ in.), Musée du Petit Palais, Geneve, Wikipedia: Public Domain.

Figure 8. Juan Gris, *Portrait of Pablo Picasso*, 1912, oil on canvas, 93.3 x 74.4 cm (36 ¾ x 29 5/16 in.), Art Institute of Chicago, Wikipedia: Public Domain.

Figure 9. Gelett Burgess, "The Wild Men of Paris," *Architectural Record*, May 1910.

Figure 10. Salon d'Automne, Salon XI, Grand Palais des Champs-Elysées, Paris, October to November 1912, Photograph: Public Domain.

Figure 11. "Salon d'Automne 1911," *The New York Times*, October 8, 1911, Wikipedia: Public Domain.

Figure 12. Juan Gris, *Houses in Paris*, 1911, oil on canvas, 52.4 x 35.2 cm (20 ⅝ x 13 ½ in.), Solomon R. Guggenheim Museum, New York, Estate of Karl Nierendorf, by purchase, Public Domain.

Figure 13. Jules Flandrin, *Portrait of Jacqueline Marval*, 1889. Wikipedia: Public Domain.

Figure 14. Jean Marchand, *La Source*, 1911, oil on canvas, 162 x 130 cm (39 ¾ x 39 ¼ in.), Wikipedia: Public Domain.

Figure 15. Roger de la Fresnaye, *The Bathers*, 1912, oil on canvas, 162 x 130 cm (63 ¾ x 51 ³⁄₁₆ in.), National Gallery of Art, Washington, D.C., Wikipedia: Public Domain.

Figure 16. Ludovic-Rodo Pissarro, *French Cancan*, c. 1906, oil on canvas, 72 x 62 cm (28 ⅜ x 24 ⅜ in.), Copyright Stern Pissarro Gallery, London.

Figure 17. Henri Le Fauconnier, *The Tree*, 1912, oil on canvas, 55.3 x 45. cm (21.7 x 17.7 in.), Frans Hals Museum, Haarlem, The Netherlands, Public Domain.

Figure 18. Ernest Ponthier de Chamaillard, *Le Chemin Creu Près du Ruisseau*, n.d., oil on canvas, 81 x 65 cm (31 ¾ x 25 ½ in.), Courtesy of Bonhams, Wikipedia: Public Domain.

Figure 19. Louis Bausil, *Wheat Field in Cerdagne,* 1903, oil on canvas, 30 x 49 cm (11 ¾ x 12 ¼ in.), Musée Hyacinth-Rigaud, Perpignan, Wikipedia: Public Domain.

Figure 20. Jacqueline Marval, *Les Odalisques*, 1902-3, oil on canvas, 166.5 x 230.7 cm (77 ¼ x 90 ¾ in.), Musée de Grenoble, Wikipedia: Public Domain. Crédit photographique : Ville de Grenoble / Musée de Grenoble-J.L. Lacroix

Figure 21. Georgette Agutte, *Marcel Sembat Reading*, c. 1900, oil on canvas, 60.5 x 49 cm (23 ¾ x 19 ¼ in.), Musée de Grenoble, Wikipedia: Public Domain. Crédit photographique : Ville de Grenoble / Musée de Grenoble-J.L. Lacroix

EDITOR'S ACKNOWLEDGEMENTS

Professor Jacqueline Gojard begins her introduction with a profound observation: "André Salmon's book *La Jeune Peinture française* (*Young French Painting*), finished in April 1912 and released on October 14ᵗʰ by the Parisian publisher Albert Messein, has had a strange fate." The same holds true for this revised and updated translation of Salmon's best-known book on early modern art in France: It has had a strange fate. We have weathered many a twist and turn in our journey to bring this volume into existence. Our most recent challenge presented itself during the first year of the Covid-19 pandemic, when our respective confinements cut off online communication for a few months. This experience reminded me of why Salmon's second book *La Jeune Sculpture française*, completed in 1914 before World War I, was not published until 1919, after the war and the influenza pandemic that took the life of his closest friend Guillaume Apollinaire. Who could have imagined one hundred years later, in 2019, that another Salmon publication would be delayed because of a similar pandemic?

Nevertheless, *la bande à Salmon* knows how to persevere, ever relentless and resilient. And the opportunity to work with Professor Gojard again, on this our third publication, remains a great honor and privilege. There is no other way to truly immerse oneself so thoroughly in Salmon's life and lore than to spend extended periods of time with Professor Gojard. Her meticulous care sets the bar high, and I am tremendously indebted to Professor Gojard for all I have learned during this project. She is our leader, our guide and our moral compass in all things Salmonian. "Merci beaucoup" cannot adequately express my gratitude.

I would like to thank the other members of *la bande à Salmon*, treasured colleagues, who have provided generous advice and support for this project and other shared Salmon endeavors: Dr. Marilena Pronesti, affiliated with the University of Turin; Dr. Franca Bruera, Full Professor of French Literature in the Department of Humanist Studies, University of Turin; and

Dr. Peter Read, Professor Emeritus of Modern French Literature and Visual Arts, University of Kent.

The first translation, published through Cambridge University Press, depended on other generous mentors, most notably Denise Gaillaguet of Rhode Island (in 1994), and Gisèle Carruth, former director of Alliance Française de Westchester in White Plains, New York (in 1999-2000). They were indeed co-translators and splendid company in this enterprise. In addition, sincere thanks go to professional translator Wendy Shefferman-Skolnik; art historian Dr. Paul Werner, director of Orange Press and *WOID: A Journal of Visual Language*; and the late art historian Marion Wolf, who read the first translation drafts of *La Jeune Peinture française* and encouraged me to strive for more fluency.

After the first translation for Cambridge University Press was published, I sent Professor Gojard the book. She gently pointed out a few errors and then eight years later agreed to collaborate on a revision. Over the last nearly forty years, Professor Gojard has generously provided me with copious resources (in particular, her own numerous articles, papers and dissertation), which were unavailable to me otherwise. Her bibliography of Salmon's works, completed with her husband Jacques Gojard, along with her essay on Salmon's nominalism, all published in *André Salmon*, number 9 *Quadarni del Novecento Francese* (1987), influenced both my doctoral dissertation and first book on Salmon's art criticism as well as this translation.

During the writing of the introduction and the notes for the first translation, Professor Gojard mailed her recent essays. Her correspondence (answering numerous questions I posed in every letter) helped me see the project through. I am infinitely grateful for her clarifications and encouragement. It is an honor to share this world of Salmon research and interpretation with her, as well as other exceptional scholars who have been sources for our work.

Along with Professor Gojard's generosity, I am greatly indebted to Professor Gojard's daughter Séverine Gojard-Desgranges, who found my email address through the internet and renewed contact between her mother and me. Thank you so much, Séverine Gojard-Desgranges, for your cordial and prompt responses.

For contributions to specific areas of inquiry, I would like to thank art historian and artist Dr. Richard Kendall, Degas specialist, who responded to my email queries regarding Salmon's Degas quotation in *La Jeune Peinture française*.

Among the libraries, I would like to thank New York Public Library, Thomas J. Watson Library at the Metropolitan Museum of Art, the Bibliothèque Nationale de Paris, the Bibliothèque Sainte-Geneviève, the Fonds Doucet, the Bibliothèque d'Art et l'Archéologie (Fondation Doucet) of the Universités de Paris, John D. Rockefeller Library at Brown University, Purchase College Library, and the Westchester Libraries System.

Another significant source has been Dr. Lynn Wissing Gamwell's dissertation on Cubist criticism. In addition, Dr. Gamwell, currently professor of art history at the School of Visual Arts, allowed me to look through her handwritten copies of Salmon's articles for my dissertation, and I am still indebted to her for those copies of articles that have bearing on his books.

There were also the opportunities to share my ideas with my peers at conferences. Thank you so much, Professor Emeritus Liana De Girolami Cheney of the University of Massachuetts Lowell, for accepting my papers on Cézannisme and Picasso's *El Guitare* for the art history panels at the Mediterranean Studies Association conferences (Aix-en-Provance in 2001 and Barcelona in 2004, respectively); thank you, Professor Benjamin Taggie of the University of Massachusetts Dartmouth and Professor Richard W. Clement of the University of Kansas, who founded the Mediterranean Studies Association and who organize the conferences, for accepting my proposals; and thank you, Dr. Alicia Craig Faxon, Professor Emeritus of Simmons College, for inviting me to join the Mediterranean Studies Association, which has provided a forum for collegial discussion over a period of several years.

I would also like to thank Professor Rose-Carol Washton Long, my dissertation advisor, who introduced me to André Salmon in her seminar on Cubism at the City University of New York Graduate and University Center and encouraged me to pursue the first translation for Cambridge University Press.

Most important of all, before there were co-translators, scholarly colleagues/consultants and anonymous internet data providers, there was Dr.

Beatrice Rehl, senior editor of Classics and Art at Cambridge University Press, who recognized the genuine need to make Salmon's work available in English and did not give up on this project through fourteen long years. Thank you, Beatrice, for your patience and support from day one.

For financial support for my Salmon projects, I am indebted to the CUNY Graduate Center in 1982 and the Mercy College Faculty Development Grant for the Spring Semester 2021.

As always, working with the extraordinarily gifted artist Ruby Silvious has been a pleasure. Her cover design captures the textual content perfectly. Najdan Mančić designed the interior to match our previous book *Pablo Picasso and André Salmon: The Painter, the Poet and the Portraits* (Za Mir Press, 2019), which is elegant and easy on the eyes. Breanna Bean and Meredith Storer proofread the text and provided excellent suggestions for the flow of the English translations. Their assistance went far beyond the tasks we initially discussed. Brad Colin's index is superb! Thank you all so much.

Finally, thank you so much Ann Cefola, Jill M. Sitkin, Veronica Nelson Dodds and Barbara Potts for listening, caring, believing in me and guiding me with your sage advice.

And above all, Dušan Nešić and Natasha Nešić, my husband and daughter, *hvala lepo*, merci beaucoup, thank you so much for putting up with me and my numerous Salmon projects all these years.

—BGN

THE TRANSLATORS' NOTES

André Salmon introduced two new expressions in his first book on art: "la jeune peinture française"[1] and "l'art vivant." These two categorical labels did not exist before this art critic coined them for his own purposes. A literal translation of these phrases cannot satisfactorily communicate the meaning Salmon infuses into their simple words.

Jeune means "young" in French, but for Salmon *jeune peinture* meant more than new or contemporary painting. "It is therefore indispensable to know, from the very beginning of this study, which artists still deserve to be considered young, either in years or as newly born sons of fame," Salmon explained to his reader. "Not only has he ceased to be the painter from these bygone eras but he has a new way of being young." In short, Salmon appeals to our understanding of youthfulness in modernist terms: fresh ideas, uninhabited drive, innovation, and rebellious zeal.

Moreover, the whole weight of this word *jeune* captures Salmon's particular anarchist spirit in relation to the arts. Youthfulness characterized Salmon's essence as a poet, critic and person. "A dreamer with an alert sensibility, he was tall, thin, distinguished, with intelligent eyes in a very pale face, and he looked very young. Nor has he changed since then," wrote Fernande Olivier in her *Picasso and His Friends*, 1933. Salmon also found young people inspired his confidence in the future.[2] This sentiment coincided with his quintessential modernist position: innovation brings progress. However, at a time when tradition and avant-gardism went head-to-head in the annual salons (mentioned

---

[1] *La jeune peinture française* was appropriated subsequently in various contexts, such as the exhibition *Le Cubism: La Jeune Peinture Française* at Gallery Moos, Geneva, Switzerland, February 1920 and Michel Charzat, *La Jeune Peinture Française, 1910-1940, une époque, un art de vivre* (Paris: Hazan Éditions, 2000).

[2] Letter to Michel Vaucaire, editor of *Le Crapouillot*, written September 22 or 24, 1924, reproduced on the blog André Salmon, Poet/Critic, December 30, 2020: https://andresalmon-poet.blogspot.com/2020/12/was-andre-salmon-jewish-non.html

in Salmon's first paragraph and listed in our notes), Salmon sought a third way through *l'art vivant*.

L'art vivant extols the positive aspects of innovation with a healthy respect for the established masters (academic and avant-garde) who paved the way. This fusion of the past, present and future should produce "l'art vivant," in English "living art," but for Salmon, so much more. *L'art vivant* means dynamic art, capable of nourishing the next generation. As Jacqueline Gojard specifically notes: "[L'art vivant is] the image/art as an organism which develops and renews itself according to the laws of an internal growth, which conflict with the socio-cultural weight of an ossified art that claims to keep up with and reside throughout the entire country." *L'art vivant* is generative art, igniting multiple responses in its wake, rather than enshrining the status quo, academic hegemony or Cubist doctrine. Thus, to maintain the unique meaning of Salmon's innovative expression *l'art vivant* (the title of his third book on art published in 1920 and a journal launched by Jacques Guenne and Martin du Gard on January 1, 1925[3]), we decided on the original French expression *l'art vivant* for the title of Salmon's third chapter, found among our colleagues' English-language publications as well.[4]

Salmon's term also fed into André Warnod's capacious moniker École de Paris (School of Paris), which corralled French and foreign artists into one modernist endeavor. However, one must not confuse the two. *L'art*

---

[3]   *L'Art vivant*, January 1, 1925, p. 3: "To Our Readers: 'Through *L'Art Vivant*, art will surely blend with life as revenge for this bloody century.' This sentence is taken from the preface of Mr. André Salmon's book which marries the lyricism of a poet to the meticulous concerns of a historian of contemporary art. This book is called *L'Art vivant*. We propose the program and activity in this epigram that is also rich in its profound meaning, and we thank the author who gave permission to our revue to introduce itself under his auspices." ("A Nos Lecteurs: 'Par L'ART VIVANT, l'art va vraiment se confondre avec la vie pour la revanche de ce siècle ensanglanté.' Cette phrase est tirée de la préface que M. André Salmon a mise à un ouvrage qui marie au lyrisme du poète le minutieux souci d'un historien de l'art contemporain. Et ce livre a pour titre *L'Art Vivant*. Proposons-nous le programme et l'activité d'une épigramme aussi riche de significations profondes, et remercions son auteur d'avoir permis à notre revue de se présenter sous ses auspices."); André Salmon, *L'Art vivant* (Paris: G. Crès et Cie, 1920).

[4]   See Christopher Green's and Kate Kangaslahti's publications cited in the bibliography.

vivant, like "*jeune*" artworks, comes from the "*esprit*" (mind and spirit) of the artists, highlighting their intentionality. École de Paris lumps together a group of international modernists who worked outside the parameters of the French academic tradition, but also outside of the more radical contemporary movements, such as Dada and Surrealism.

In 1912, Salmon invented the term *l'art vivant* for the emerging independent moderns, whose work was neither Fauve nor Cubist, and yet demonstrated great promise because of its individualist aesthetic choices. Most of the descriptions written in *La Jeune Peinture française* come from Salmon's regular art review column "Courriers des Ateliers," published in the daily newspaper *Paris-Journal* from 1910 through 1911. By 1920, having survived a devastating war and pandemic, the notion of a "living art" took on a more resonant quality. Salmon's third book on art, *L'Art vivant,* based again on his newspaper art reviews published in *Montjoie!* and elsewhere, graduates the "young" artists from the state of emerging to the position of masters taking over the art world through their vitality and uncompromising dedication to pushing boundaries. In his poem on painting: *Peindre* (1921), Salmon set down the fundamentals of *l'art vivant*:

> *Peindre, c'est imiter l'imitation,*
> *Seul secret si tu dois recréer la nature*
> *Et ne rien imiter*
> *Que de l'illimité*
> *Dans l'ordre et la mesure*

> *Painting means to imitate the imitation,*
> *The only secret, if you must re-create nature,*
> *Imitate nothing*
> *But its boundlessness*
> *Through order and moderation.*
> — BGN and JG

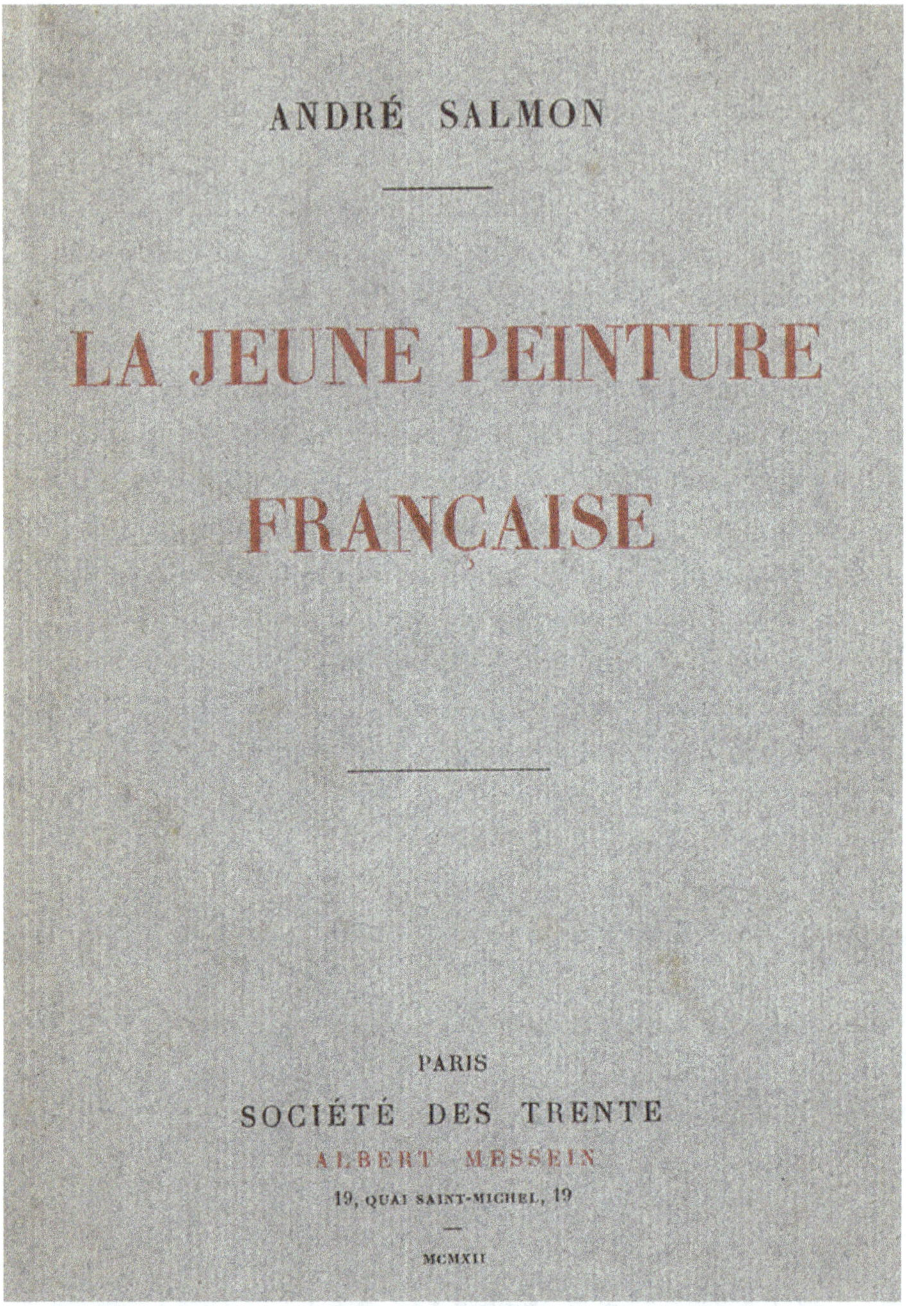

ANDRÉ SALMON

LA JEUNE PEINTURE

FRANÇAISE

PARIS

SOCIÉTÉ DES TRENTE

ALBERT MESSEIN

19, QUAI SAINT-MICHEL, 19

MCMXII

Figure 1. Cover of *La Jeune Peinture française*, Paris: Société des Trente, Albert Messein, 1912.

ON PICASSO, SALMON AND *YOUNG FRENCH PAINTING*

by Jacqueline Gojard

André Salmon's book *La Jeune Peinture française* (*Young French Painting*), finished in April 1912 and released on October 14 by the Parisian publisher Albert Messein, has had a strange fate. A century has passed without producing a new edition in France, and the text remains almost unavailable for the interested researcher. Moreover, the work has been cited in numerous studies on early twentieth-century painting, including monographs and analyses of Fauvism, Cubism and the birth of the School of Paris. Some chapters, such as "Histoire anecdotique du cubisme" ("The Anecdotal History of Cubism"), have been translated several times[5] to the detriment of the whole book and the role of Salmon as the source and guide for a public not counted among the "happy few" in the contemporary art world. At last, in 2005, *André Salmon on French Modern Art* (Cambridge University Press), a translation into English by Beth S. Gersh-Nešić paired *Young French Painting* and its "younger sibling" *La Jeune Sculpture française* (*Young French Sculpture*)—written in 1914 and published in 1919, also by Albert Messein. Accompanied by a preface and annotations, this combination permits the reader to envision how Salmon (a poet born in the same month and year as his close friend Pablo Picasso,

---

5 Edward Fry, *Cubism*, translations from French and German by Jonathan Griffin (London: Thames and Hudson, 1966), 81–90; Herschel B. Chipp with Peter Selz and Joshua C. Taylor, *Theories of Modern Art*, translations by Herschel B. Chipp (Berkeley: University of California, 1968), 199–206; Mark Antliff and Patricia Leighten, eds., *A Cubism Reader: Documents and Criticism*, translations from French by Jane Marie Todd (Chicago: University of Chicago, 2008), 357–367 ("Anecdotal History of Cubism"); 370–375 ("Feminine Painting in the Twentieth Century").

October 1881) contributed through his writing to the careers of young artists who came to Paris to make their mark during the decade before World War I.

The attentive reader of *Young French Painting* cannot help asking questions closely tied to the paradoxical fate referred to above. Why did Salmon focus his book on the birth of a work (the future *Demoiselles d'Avignon*) at a time when it was unknown and never exhibited in public? Why did he choose the Spanish Pablo Picasso as a "prince" for his *Young French Painting*? Isn't there an obvious contradiction between the first half of the text's distinctive avant-garde choices and the second half's advocacy of both boldness and restraint with a feeling for innovation and respect for some traditionalism? Why risk mentioning nearly one hundred young painters when it would have been safer to restrict praise to a dozen names that were already anointed by fame or crowned by controversy?

Nothing seems stranger than Salmon's choices, which are compared to those of his colleague and friend Guillaume Apollinaire whose *Méditations esthétiques* (*Esthetic Meditations*) appeared in 1913, published under the title *Les Peintres cubistes* (*The Cubist Painters*) by Figuière. After a series of theoretical generalizations, buttressed by his powerfully lyrical tone, Apollinaire set forth his attempt to classify Cubism according to four tendencies: scientific, physical, orphic and instinctive. Then he juxtaposed nine brief essays dedicated to Picasso, Georges Braque, Jean Metzinger, Albert Gleizes, Mademoiselle Marie Laurencin, Juan Gris, Fernand Léger, Francis Picabia and Marcel Duchamp—painters gathered together, for better or worse, under the Cubist label. Thus, he provoked violent polemics that, rather than damaging him, immediately legitimized his role as the self-proclaimed defender of the avant-garde.

Without expecting to answer the questions raised by *Young French Painting*, we can at least try today to examine it more clearly, taking into account the risks Salmon incurred and the profits he reaped as compensation.

Let us begin with the case of *Les Demoiselles d'Avignon*. Most critics who read the chapter "Anecdotal History of Cubism" from the perspective of Picasso claim that Salmon did not like the painting and then derisively called it *Le Bordel philosophique* (*The Philosophical Brothel*). Didn't he himself admit that he was frozen with horror by the hideous faces of these figures? His first reaction was one of the "half-converted": The poets and painters who frequented the Bateau-Lavoir (Apollinaire, Max Jacob, Derain and Braque) missed the immediate seductiveness of the Rose Period and thought that this new direction was dangerous, even suicidal.

Can we now understand why, at this point, Salmon dedicated a dozen pages more to this work, instead of ignoring it like Apollinaire who never breathed a word about it? And wasn't it pure folly to want to interest the 1912 reader in a canvas that still hadn't left the artist's studio? Further, since this was about the genesis of the experiment, why would the public care about the previous states of a work that had never been seen?

This was indeed Salmon's choice—to talk about something unknown and unknowable. It doesn't matter that we know whether he liked the painting or not, but that we understand why he accorded it a unique place and treatment in his *Young French Painting*, agreeing with Picasso—in contrast to the little clan of the "half-converted."

An assiduous reader of Rimbaud since his adolescence and an unconditional admirer of *Une saison en enfer* (*A Season in Hell*), perhaps he was better suited to stand up for a complete aesthetic rupture and applaud a "loose cannon," which happened to disturb the already smoothly run mechanisms of anti-cultural practices. According to Rimbaud, an art "resolutely modern" could not submit to the old European values of the beautiful and the good; it had to be rethought in terms of energy. For Salmon, Picasso was to painting what Rimbaud had been to poetry: "No concern about grace; taste repudiated as a very narrow measure." Moreover, with his "philosophical brothel," he had stood up to all the principles of authority. At the price of a veritable orgy of energy, he had created a work capable of regenerating himself, and, at the same time, all painting.

After following the development of the canvas "step by step" as if it were a "military proving ground," Salmon praised Picasso's effort to situate his "balanced figures outside the laws of academicism and an anatomical system in a space rigorously conforming to the unforeseen freedom of their movements." He overcame his doubts to affirm that "the decision to create in such a way is enough to make the person who pursues it the foremost artist of his time." He had the intuition that "the hideousness of the faces" contributed to the very power of Picasso's first gesture: *Les Demoiselles* ended the reign of the *Mona Lisa* whose smile "was perhaps the Sun of Art for too long." And the reference to Rimbaud came so naturally to Salmon's pen! Remembering the famous exclamation in poem "Les Premières Communions" ("First Communions"): "Christ! Oh Christ, eternal thief of energies," he wrote: "One could say, paraphrasing Arthur Rimbaud, that the *Mona Lisa*, the eternal *Mona Lisa*, was the thief of energies."

Because he thought like a poet, Salmon made Picasso the hero of his book. One evening "through a sublime caprice," the painter had, he tells us, crowned with roses the portrait of a young worker—the famous *Boy with a Pipe* (1906). With the same casualness, the author of *Young French Painting* bestows the title of "prince" on his Spanish friend, challenging Matisse, the "king of the Fauves." Salmon had, himself, lived abroad for five years (1896–1901) in Saint Petersburg, one of the most cosmopolitan cities in Europe. The nationalistic spirit that infected so many compatriots since Germany's victory in 1871 and the convulsive scenario of the Dreyfus Affair of 1894–1906 were alien to him. He thought that France's honor was to greet artists who had come to enrich his native culture. In turn, he supported with equal enthusiasm the foreign artists of the School of Paris (Modigliani, Juan Gris, Chagall, Soutine, Kisling, Pascin and Foujita).

Partial to creative artists, he proved to be, on the other hand, critical of followers, false naïve artists, late-blooming Fauves and late converts to Cubism. The arguments among the schools, conflicts about precedents and paternity, the frantic quest of die-hard modernity offered nothing of value to him. Cubism interested him as a spiritual adventure, a new configuration of objects in space, which broke with mimetic norms, but not as a pictorial dogma. He called attention to anywhere he found Living Art and preferred to anyone else the youthful, independent painter who maintained a precarious balance, like a tightrope walker, between the desire to innovate (which activates the hand) and the research for order of any kind—as long as it ensures mastery over the picture. When one translates the text of *Young French Painting*, one has to mobilize all the arsenal of concessive grammatical structures (such as "yet," "however," "nevertheless," etc.), which act as a pendulum. For Salmon positioned himself equidistant from the clichés of tradition and those of the avant-garde. Energy, audacity, rigor, and authenticity were the key words in his book. Whoever lived up to these qualities was worthy of being mentioned.

There are two ways to envision an artistic period: Either one chooses the leading, valiant avant-garde figures, worthy of entering someday into the Heaven of the Greats (the Louvre), which was what Apollinaire had in mind for his *Cubists Painters*. Or one can paint a larger picture by presenting multiple efforts and tendencies, in the spirit of openness (as we see in the Musée d'Orsay), that do not overlap areas of study where borders continue to shift. That is what Salmon did in *Young French Painting*—particularly in the last three chapters. When he advocates for the artists of minor repute, when he hopes for a decentralized politics and a renaissance of fresco in art and says the official orders should be offered to the young artists rather than the members of the Institute de France, he seems to say: "Let them in." His discourse is not meant to appoint himself as a hegemonic critic for this moment in modernity. He wants to offer a fighting chance to those who are struggling "in the mêlée" by giving them a helping hand.

No doubt he risked naming the painters whom posterity would not remember well. If one takes into consideration the fact that a certain number of these artists died prematurely, victims of World War I, one notices that the segment of painters who have fallen into oblivion is relatively small and tends to decrease in size as our knowledge about this period increases. By generously mentioning about one hundred artists, Salmon deserves, above all, praise for reviving an epoch when everything was "interconnected." The poets and the painters met in studios and cafés in Montmartre and Montparnasse, at Leo and Gertrude Stein's home on 27 rue de Fleurus. They went to Chatelet to applaud the Ballets Russes and participated in the *orientale* parties hosted by the couturier Paul Poiret. The city was covered with posters, and the artists saw in these decorative arts a way to escape from easel painting and the confined space of the galleries and the museum. Salmon brought the reader along on this adventure. His book contains some factual errors, sometimes irritating prejudices (against Matisse, for example), which may be of greater value than some soothing eclecticism. Also, some errors come from perspective, due to the date of the writing. Neither Dufy, Picabia nor Duchamp were in April 1912 the artist we know today. And Braque still had not invented *papier collé*, which offered new possibilities to Cubism. It doesn't matter. Salmon's criticism did not claim to be scientific. Lively, complex and sometimes contradictory, it was always stimulating. It enthusiastically presented to us, not without a touch of irony here and there, "the golden age of painting" in France.

All said and done, on balance the book—such as it is with all its weakness and inevitable mistakes in judgment—can be viewed in a decidedly positive light.

Salmon won the bet he placed on the *Demoiselles* a long time ago, and the author of *Young French Painting* himself greatly contributed to this outcome. As an ex-soldier back from the trenches, he returned to Paris in the spring of 1916 after staying in various military hospitals, and then he spent a few months organizing the exhibition "L'Art Moderne en France" (also called the Salon d'Antin), which was held from July 16 through July 31 at 26 rue d'Antin, a location that Paul Poiret made available to him. Most of the artists mentioned in the 1912 book are in the 1916 catalogue beside some newcomers, such as De Chirico, Kisling and Modigliani, among others. "Picasso (Spanish)" participated as No. 129 with his *Demoiselles d'Avignon*, a "decent" title invented by Salmon to avoid attacks from the censors, who were stricter than ever during the war. Despite the hostile reactions of the critics, at this point the painting began its career, conferring upon the chapter "Anecdotal History of Cubism" its incontrovertible value as a reference for those who study the genesis of this masterpiece and its on-the-spot reception, which was limited to an audience of friends at the Bateau-Lavoir.

For a long time, this chapter has been examined under a magnifying glass, or like the tree hiding the forest. Today, we are no longer condemned to such short-sightedness. We can read it in its original context, in this translation of *La Jeune Peinture française* (*Young French Painting*), an incomparable eyewitness to the artistic fecundity of the early twentieth century.

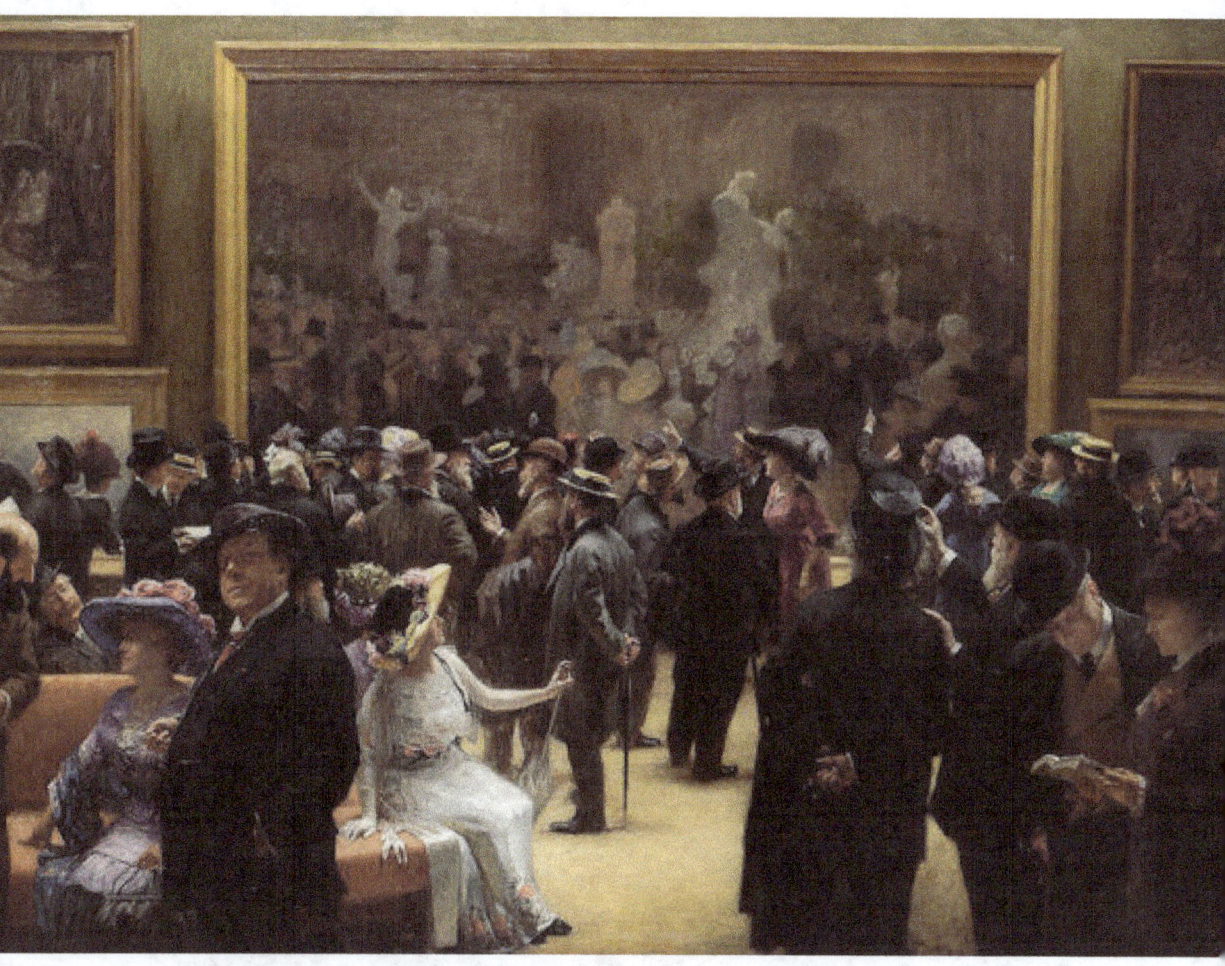

Figure 2. Henri Adolphe Laissement (1854-1921) *Salon of French Artists in 1911*, 1911-12, Private Collection

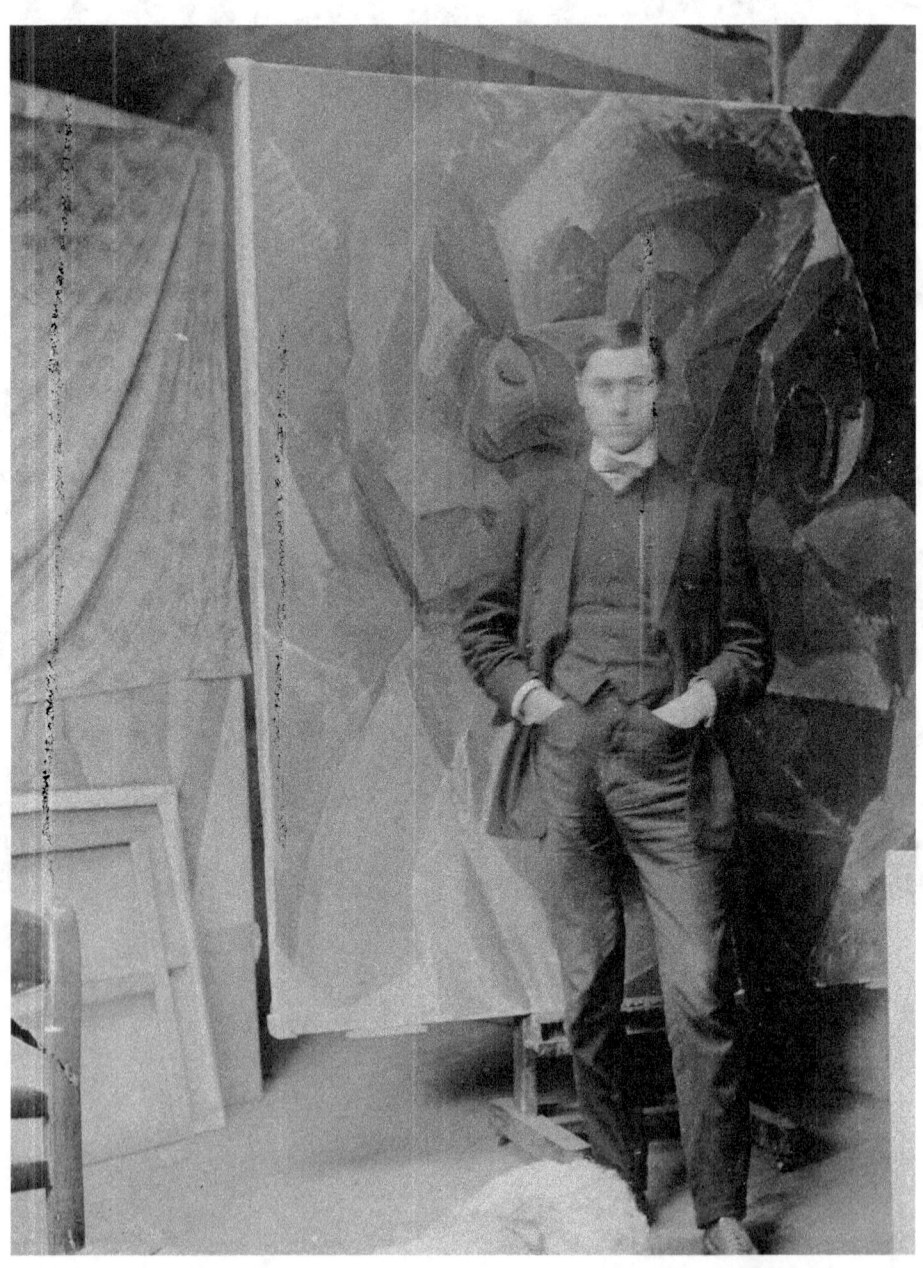

André Salmon in front of Picasso's *Three Women* in Picasso's studio, 1908

FOREWORD

Based on statistics gathered over several years, the Paris art season (October to the end of June) is crammed with at least twelve salons, ten retrospectives, forty art society exhibitions and about one hundred private exhibitions, which are important enough to receive reviews by well-known critics.[6] If this is the case, one can assume that the public is sufficiently acquainted with contemporary painting. Therefore, although taking on this task, I will not present the whole picture. Such a slim volume would not suffice. Nor will I try to define the latest trend in painting, as others have already.[7]

Instead, I will try (with a simplicity that I dare to believe might be appreciated) to put a bit of order into much confusion, to uncover authentic origins, to define more precisely certain misunderstood aspirations, to reveal

---

[6] There were four great official exhibitions at that time: Salon d'Automne (begun 1903); Salon des Indépendants (begun 1884); Salon de la Société Nationale des Beaux-Arts (begun 1890); Salon des Artistes Français (begun 1673). They were known as "L'Automne," "Les Indépendants," "La Nationale," and "Les Artistes Français." There were many specialized ones, such as the Salon d'hiver (founded in 1897); Salon de l'École Française (begun 1903); Salon de l'Union des Femmes Peintres et Sculpteurs (begun 1881); Salon des Arts Décoratifs (begun 1905); Salon des Aquarellistes (begun 1878); Salon des Graveurs (begun 1900); Salon des Humoristes (begun 1908); Salon de la Comédie Humaine (begun 1906). [BGN/JG]

[7] Salmon wrote "le dernier état de la peinture," which refers directly to Michel Puy's essay "Le Dernier État de la peinture," *Mercure de France*, July 16, 1910, 243–266, published as a book in 1911 and then included (along with other essays) in *L'Effort des peintres modernes* (Paris: Albert Messein, 1933)—the publisher of *La Jeune peinture française*. Apollinaire reviewed Puy's book for *L'Intransigeant*, February 14, 1911. Other possible references may be to Jean Metzinger's "Note sur la peinture," *Pan!* (Paris), October–November 1910, 649–52; Olivier-Hourcade's "La Tendance de la peinture contemporaine (notes pour une causerie sur l'art contemporain)," *Revue de France et des Pays français*, February 1912, 35–41; Jacques Rivière's "Sur les tendances actuelles de la peinture," *Revue d'Europe et d'Amérique*, March 1, 1912, 384–406; and Guillaume Apollinaire's, "La Peinture Nouvelle: Notes d'art," *Les Soirées de Paris*, no. 3 (April 1912): 89–92; and no. 4 (May 1912): 113–115.

some affiliations, and to create (through local associations) families of artists, since—strictly speaking—there are no longer any schools.

Above all, I will try to summarize the artistic history of the last few years.

I will provide irrefutable proof (if memory serves me well), having had the good fortune to attend a few births, interrupt various retirements, bear witness at close range and be among the first in the know.

Innovators (art's revolutionaries) have the unique privilege of upsetting some norms, indeed as formidable as the social order itself—without the public batting an eye.

When the *Fédérés* set fire to the Tuileries in May, it did not go unnoticed; so, they were shot without delay.[8] And yet, a vast majority of ignorant people will not discover (and condemn) the finest Impressionists until the Camondo bequest is finally put on display.[9]

---

[8]   The insurrection of the Paris Commune, following the fall of France defeated by the Prussians, lasted a very short time (March to May 1871) and resulted in a blood bath. "More French were killed during 'Bloody Week' (May 21–28) than during the Reign of Terror or the Prussian Siege," according to Albert Boime in *Art and the French Commune: Imagining Paris after War and Revolution* (Princeton: Princeton University Press, 1995), 5. Salmon's remark refers to the burning of the Tuileries Palace, instigated on May 23rd by the insurgents, known as les *Fédérés*. The palace, the former royal and imperial residence, situated behind the Arc du Carrousel and connected to the Louvre through a series of galleries, burned for three days (leaving behind the place which today is part of the Tuileries Garden). During these final days of the Commune, there were about fifty thousand arrests and thirty thousand deaths of Parisians/Communards defending themselves against the Versailles Government, led by Louis-Adolphe Thiers, president of the Third Republic. (Boime, 4) [BGN] Salmon's parents participated in the Commune and had to go into exile in London in order escape repression after "Bloody Week." [JG] Here Salmon compares the political rebellion of the Commune in 1871 to the artistic rebellion of the Impressionist in 1874. The former was attacked and squelched immediately. The latter remained unnoticed by a large portion of the population almost forty years later. [BGN]

[9]   Isaac de Camondo (1851–1911) amassed a considerable collection of art including several masterpieces by Manet (*Lola de Valence*, *The Fifer*), Monet (four paintings of Rouen Cathedral and two of his water lilies paintings), Degas (*Woman Ironing*, *Absinthe Drinkers*, *The Tub*), Sisley (*The Flood at Port Marly*), Cézanne (*The Hanged Man's House*, *The Card Players*), Boudin and Jongkind. He bequeathed his collection to the Louvre in 1908. The collection entered the Louvre in 1911 and was put on view together in 1914. These works are now part of the Musée d'Orsay's permanent collection. [BGN]

Wasn't it only at the Louvre Courbet's *Burial at Ornans* and Manet's *Olympia* could really shock decent society?[10]

Nonetheless, the wide variety of exhibitions (which serve as fodder for old French wit) facilitate a quicker discovery of the painter born under a cursed star.

It is therefore indispensable to know, from the very beginning of this study, which artists still deserve to be considered young, either in years or as newly born sons of fame.

That's easy enough. First, let's consider the precursors, living or dead, the blessed souls whose mortal work has been judged and admitted into national or municipal Heaven—better known as the museums.

Next, we find the souls (and here we mean the rebels) destined for immortality, and yet their trial on earth is still not over.

Finally, there are the agitated and tangled up bodies that must be approached one by one. Of these, we can only imagine their eternal fate.

These are the ones who will be of particular interest to me.

The young French painter of 1912 is surprisingly different from the young French painter of the Renaissance, from the republican student of David's day, from the Jeune-France *rapin,* or from the Anatole in that tedious novel, *Manette Salomon.*[11]

---

[10] Gustave Courbet's *Burial in Ornans* (1850) was a gift to the Louvre from the artist's sister Juliette Courbet in 1881. It was on display at the Louvre from 1882 to 1986, whereupon it was transferred to the Musée d'Orsay. The museum opened in December. Manet's *Olympia* (1863) was acquired through a public subscription organized by Claude Monet in 1890. The painting hung in the Musée du Luxembourg from 1890 to 1907, from 1907 to 1947 in the Louvre, and from 1947 to 1986 in the Jeu de Paume. In 1986, *Olympia* was transferred to the Musée d'Orsay. I would like to thank the Musée d'Orsay for this information. [BGN]

[11] A *rapin* was usually a new student in an art studio whose responsibilities included arriving early to warm up the stove, sweep the floor, tidy up the room, wash the brushes, etc. *Rapin* also meant an advanced student who showed little promise. Les Jeunes-France were rebellious young artists and writers of the 1830s Romantic Period, who dressed in exotic clothes and adopted a mannered behavior inspired by the middle ages. (Also refer to note 18.) *Manette Salomon* was a novel written by Edmond and Jules de Goncourt; published in 1867, it was about contemporary life among French artists. Anatole, a young painter, is one of the main characters. [BGN]

Not only has he ceased to be the painter from these bygone eras, but he has a new way of being young. His character transformations are more substantial than merely frivolous outward appearances. Later on I will cite some painters—among the most intelligent of the group—who claim that they no longer paint. Yet, these artists say that with palettes in their hands.

May their attitude be my justification. They are like me, a man of letters who, everyone knows, should not take on the role of art critic.

Therefore, I do not intend to play the role of a Godlike judge, who presides over minor court cases with fair-minded goodwill, distributing acquittals or condemnations.

I will play the role of historian, but not according to the modern formula that satisfies the love of gossip and news briefs. I may also be a geographer and, consequently, a politician when it comes to defining or modifying national borders, without any compensation.

To carry out one's duty under these circumstances is not easy; the secret complicity of the reader is indispensable. He to whom we address ourselves is a good servant of art, and loves both old and modern painting with all his heart.

. . . the first love after the love of God![12]

In some articles written for the daily newspapers,[13] I have on occasion defended painters whom I did not like very much. I made myself their advocate after a compassionate study of their accomplishments because I knew that they were sincere and nobly concerned, and that it was important to save them from the laughter of drunken gawkers.

Today I know that I address myself to a select gathering. I am no longer pleading a case, but simply offering a report.

---

[12]   In the original ". . . Le premier amour après l'amour de Dieu" Salmon parodies two verses by Paul Verlaine, which he condenses into one: "L'amour de la patrie est le premier amour/Et le dernier amour après l'amour de Dieu," *Bonheur*, XXX, Vanier, 1891. "Love of country is the first love/And the last after the love of God." [JG]

[13]   Salmon refers to his critiques in two important daily newspapers: *L'Intransigeant* and *Paris-Journal*. [JG]

After this address to the reader, a word to the painters of whom we will speak.

Permit me at the beginning of this book to praise a masterful liberator to whom as much is owed as to Delacroix, Courbet, Manet, Renoir, Seurat, Toulouse-Lautrec, van Gogh, Degas, Cézanne, etc.

Namely, Odilon Redon.

Though illustrious, he is hardly more famous than Stéphane Mallarmé had been during his lifetime.[14]

Yet the glory of this great artist will remain as eternally pure as that of the poet of *Hérodiade*.[15]

Like him for whom the transparency of a coffee cup inspired a miraculous sonnet,[16] Odilon Redon paints "still lifes" which move us like wondrous visions.

Happy are those who perceive the fragrance and savor the quality of his flowers!

Odilon Redon has nothing of the sorcerer about him. This magnificent painter is a hospitable and gentle old man, a French bourgeois from the grand tradition. He does not have a studio; instead, he paints in a little, modestly furnished and brightly lit sitting-room.[17] The noise of the electric trams, which run on the avenue below, does not disturb the serenity of his dream. The

---

[14] Stéphane Mallarmé died in 1898 and Odilon Redon in 1916. [BGN]

[15] This dramatic poem, written by Mallarmé in 1865 is considered one of the masterpieces of "pure poetry." [JG] Joris-Karl Huysmans introduced Redon and Mallarmé to each other around 1882–83, according to John Reward, *Post-Impressionism: From van Gogh to Gauguin* (New York: Museum of Modern Art/Boston: New York Graphic Society, 3rd ed. 1978), 165. [BGN]

[16] The sonnet is "Placet futile" ("A Futile Petition") in *Poésies*, 1887. Mallarmé invokes a Sèvres porcelaine cup with a pastoral scene decoration that stirs up an erotic revery: Mallarmé would like to be the little shepherd caressed by his ladylove as he brings the cup to his lips. [JG]

[17] Redon moved into a spacious apartment at 129 avenue de Wagram, Paris, in April 1905. He sold the family estate, Peyrelebade in 1897. Redon died at home at the age of 76. (Roseline Bacou, *Odilon Redon: Pastels*. Translated by Beatrice Rehl. (New York: George Braziller, 1987), 184. [BGN]

least pure among artists and the worst among the *Bousingots*[18] are profoundly shocked by ordinary modernism, while others—a Mallarmé, a Moréas,[19] a Redon—rise above it so effortlessly!

Odilon Redon no longer exhibits willingly. He works patiently for himself and for a few admirers. Marveling at the increasing number of exhibitions, he good-naturedly, and without the slightest resentment, recalls that in his youth even the best artists would not be placed in a corner of a window on the rue Laffitte.[20] "Today," he says, "is the golden age of painting!"

This master is one of the most undisputed emancipators. Thirty years before the term was coined, he made "pure painting," and I doubt that without his discoveries as a colorist, Fauvism (already dated but still rich) would have ever come to pass.

If painters, like poets, adopted the custom of electing a Prince,[21] it would befit them to elevate to such a sovereign position Odilon Redon, that magnificent solitary soul.

---

[18]   The word *bousingot* comes from a nineteenth-century leather sailor's cap worn by volunteers from Le Havre who came to the rescue of Paris in 1830. The word may also come from the word *bousin*, which means brouhaha or commotion. The *Bousingot* refers to a politically radical type, usually a student, who wore working-class clothes and espoused liberal political positions, often demonstrating in the streets. Their contemporaries, les Jeunes-France (see note 11), adopted their own medievalized fashion statements, grew beards and wore long hair. These two counterculture types from the early 1830s are often mentioned together in today's literature on Romantic poseurs and are usually considered interchangeable. Among the *Bousingots* were Romantic literary figures Théophile Gautier (who wrote a book of reminiscences entitled *Les Jeunes France*, published in 1833), Gérard de Nerval, Petrus Borel, etc. [BGN]

[19]   The Greco-French poet Jean Moréas (1856–1910) was one of the leading members of the literary circle that met at La Closerie des Lilas in Montparnasse, which Salmon and his friends participated in as well. [JG]

[20]   The rue Laffitte was known as the place for avant-garde artists, like Cézanne, van Gogh, Gauguin, etc. In 1912, Durand-Ruel, Bernheim-Jeune, and Ambroise Vollard had their galleries on that street. [JG]

[21]   Paul Fort was elected Prince of Poets in August 1912, succeeding Paul Verlaine, Stéphane Mallarmé and Léon Dierx. [JG]

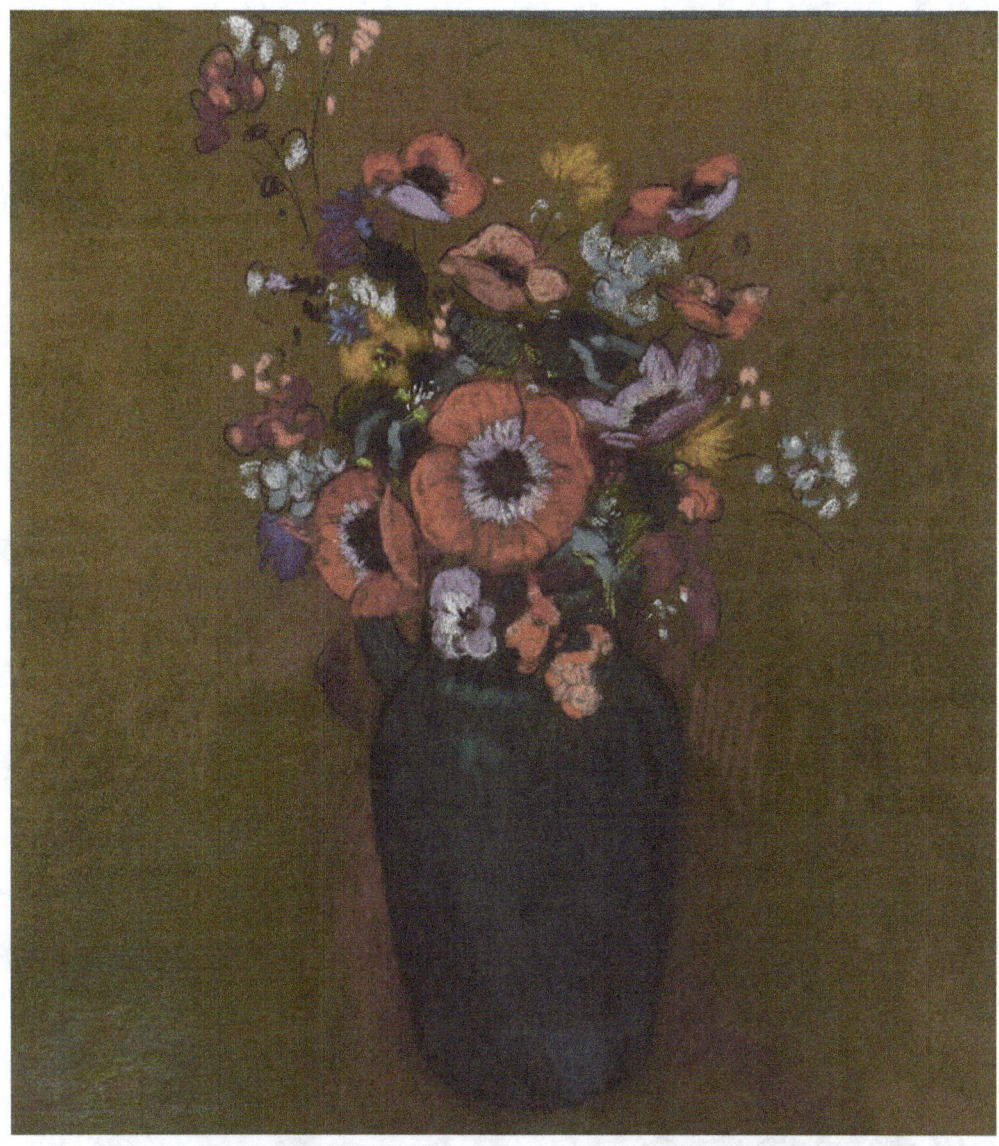

Figure 3. Odilon Redon, *Vase of Flowers*, 1900-1910
Princeton University Art Museum

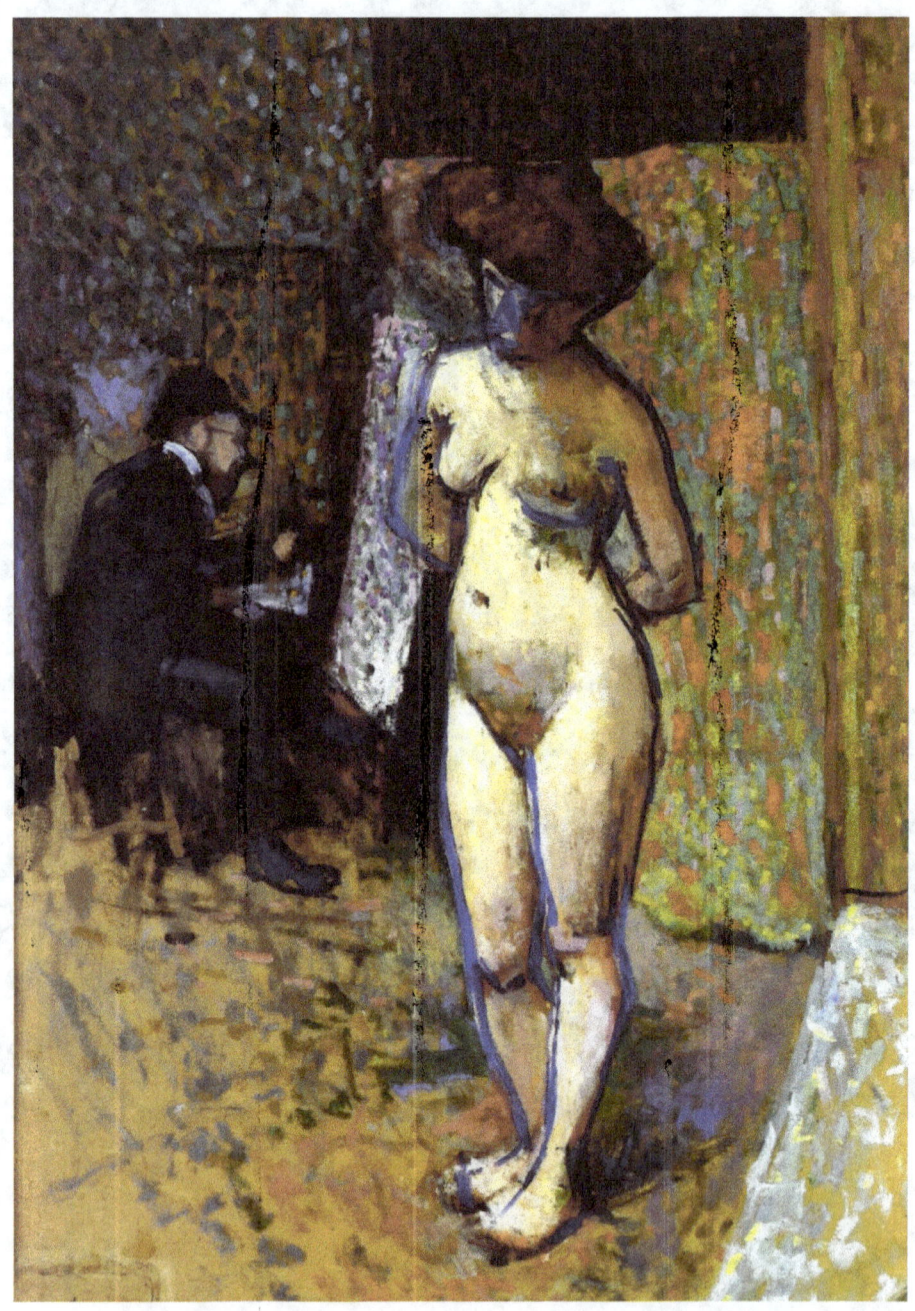

Figure 4. Albert Marquet, *Matisse in Manguin's Studio*, 1905

1

The Fauves

Pointillism was no longer shocking. The French Artists' Salon was becoming a refuge for Impressionism, which was tolerated by those moderates like an inoffensive radicalism.[22] Bonnard and Vuillard might insult only a few art-lovers from the suburbs, while the others, former

---

[22] In December 1880, the Société des Artistes Français assumed the responsibility for mounting the annual Salon (Official Exhibition of Living Artists), run by the French government from 1726 to 1880. Edmund Turquet signed the decree and established the society (Jane Mayo Roos, *Early Impressionism and the French State (1866–1874)* [Cambridge: Cambridge University Press, 1996], 222–223). [BGN] This society, founded at the end of the seventeenth century, reunited the most conservative painters, trained in the tradition of the École des Beaux-Arts. At first quite hostile toward the Impressionists, the members of its jury ended up welcoming them in their annual salon where they took on the role of the "radicals" (the Reformist and moderate arm of the political Left in France). [JG]

readers of *La Revue blanche,* found endless charm in their intellectual "*villégiatures.*"[23]

The atmosphere was one of general acceptance: Cézanne and Gauguin were commercialized. Young Danish or American ladies discovered Tahiti on the Ile de Groix,[24] and several of Madeleine Lemaire's students successfully mastered the celebrated three apples, so many of which came to us from Aix-en-Provence.[25]

Was it the failure of salutary violence? Were the revolutionaries becoming middle class?

They were, quite simply, a bit weary, exhausted by having lived under too many directions for so many years—begging from Toulouse-Lautrec and Signac, Cézanne and Gauguin, Vincent van Gogh and Maurice Denis, one after another.

---

[23] *La Revue blanche,* founded by Alexandre, Thaddeus and Louis Alfred Natanson, started in Liège in 1889, moved to Paris in 1891 and ceased publication in 1903 (before the infamous "cage aux fauves" at the Salon d'automne in 1905). Here Salmon refers to its association with the Post-Impressionists/Intimists and Nabi members Pierre Bonnard (1867–1947) and Édouard Vuillard (1868–1940) who were regarded as the avant-garde in their day. (For more information on Vuillard and the Natanson family, read Stephen Brown, "An Artist, His Patrons and the Muses," in Édouard Vuillard [New Haven, CT: Yale Press/New York: Jewish Museum, 2012], 1–75. [BGN]) The readers of *La Revue blanche* were former Communards, anarchists' sympathizers and solid Dreyfusards; they idolized Stéphane Mallarmé, Claude Debussy and Paul Gauguin. Vuillard followed his dear Misia (Thadée Natanson's wife, better known as Misia Sert from her third marriage to Spanish painter José-Marie Sert) to the family's country estate Le Relais in Villeneuve-sur-Yonne during seasonal vacations (so-called *villégiatures*), while Bonnard joined Paul Signac in Saint-Tropez. From those vacations they brought back luminous and serene paintings which delighted the art lovers. [JG]

[24] The Ile de Groix is off the southern coast of Brittany, not far from Le Pouldu, made famous in Gauguin's paintings. [BGN]

[25] Madeleine Lemaire (1845–1928) was a well-known French watercolorist whose salon and atelier received some of the most noted luminaries in the arts, letters and politics, such as Marcel Proust. Aix-en-Provence refers to Paul Cézanne (1839–1906), who was born, lived most of his life and died there. [BGN]

The latter refused to be put at the head of a new movement. In the meantime, throughout this period, all his authority endured. Félix Vallotton contemplated Cabanel.[26]

Without a chief, an army nevertheless organized itself in the dark, and even though they were not recognized right away, some of them discovered that they were fated to be leaders.

Several groups formed. If the undersecretary of the Beaux-Arts had his brigade of so-called anarchists, they would have searched with more success at Matisse's or Picasso's studios than at any other time—and for other *motifs*, at the good Maximilien Luce's.[27]

They conspired in Montmartre, Chatou, the quai Saint-Michel, and in one humble dairy store on the rue Saint-Louis-en-l'Isle.

Picasso and van Dongen hung out in Montmartre, where Georges Braque would join them. André Derain and Vlaminck wandered around Chatou. Marquet would meet the novelist Charles-Louis-Philippe, his neighbor from the Cité, on the rue Saint-Louis-en-l'Isle. The writer provided the painter with unique models: shady guys and floozies, regular fixtures in the barbarian splendor of those music bars, quite similar to the fancy carousels with all their wooden horses—so that one need not feel drunk to believe they are spinning on a chrysoprase pole.

---

[26] Félix Vallotton (1867–1925) was a member of the Post-Impressionist group called the Nabis, followers of Gauguin. Alexandre Cabanel (1823–1889) was a popular academic painter during the 1860s. *Birth of Venus*, 1863 (now in the Musée d'Orsay, in Paris; another version is in the Metropolitan Museum of Art, in New York), is among his best-known works. [BGN/JG]

[27] Here the word *motif* may be translated as both motif and motive—a typical example of wordplay for Salmon and his cronies. The Neo-Impressionist Maximilien Luce was called a "dangerous anarchist" by Adolphe Tabarant in his review "Impressions quotidiennes," *La Petite République*, December 16, 1894, 1. Luce was arrested in connection with the Procès des Trente of 1894, one of several government actions to suppress anarchism (John G. Hutton, *Neo-Impressionism and the Search for Solid Ground: Art, Science, and Anarchism in Fin-de-Siècle France* [Baton Rouge: Louisiana State University Press, 1994], 2–3, 49–50). [BGN]

Strolling in this way from le Sébasto[28] to Les Halles, Marquet brought back an admirable series of pastels, as beautiful as those by Degas but more tragic (a more concentrated vision, too), which were truly the first impressions of a modern crowd.

Charles-Louis-Philippe offered them to a bookseller who was reprinting his *Bubu de Montparnasse.* The publisher became very angry, preferring the mediocre sketches of a young man (full of good intentions but not gifted by the gods) to Marquet's unique compositions.[29]

Perhaps this defeat for Marquet was a blessing in disguise. In any case, the artist was not discouraged. He went back alone, having learned from Philippe his way through the oldest Parisian streets, and his vision of the urban landscape became broader each day. Now he is celebrated.[30]

Finally, Matisse came along![31]

Matisse, who was the first to become prince and head of a school, attracted the Normand Othon Friesz and André Derain to his atelier on the quai

---

[28] An abbreviation for the Boulevard Sébastopol, one of the places in Paris frequented by shady fellows and easy girls on the make. [JG]

[29] Salmon commented on this "Bubu Affair" (which resulted in the 1905 publication by Édition Albin Michel, with ninety illustrations by Jean Grandjouan), in his *Souvenirs sans fin* (Gallimard, repr. 2004), 153: "this Grandjouan whose skill is a far cry from Marquet's talent." [JG]

[30] In 1904, Charles-Louis Philippe (1874–1909) suggested to Marquet that he illustrate the reprint of his novel *Bubu de Montparnasse* (1901). During the summer, Marquet wrote to Matisse that he was busy with the *Bubu* illustrations, and on September 11, 1904, he wrote again to say that "Bubu, cette fois, est tout à fait mort." ("This time, Bubu is completely dead.") The editor, Mr. de Noussane, without looking at Marquet's work, gave the commission to the artist for the satirical review *L'Assiette au beurre*, Jean Grandjouan. (Michèle Paret, "Biographie," in *Albert Marquet: du fauvisme à l'impressionnisme* exhibition catalogue [Paris: Musée national d'art moderne, Centre Pompidou/Troyes: Musée d'Art moderne de Troyes, 2003] 101–102). [BGN]

[31] A parody of a fragment in *L'Art poétique* by Boileau in 1674 (Song I, v. 131) that all French school children memorize: "Enfin Malherbe vint, et, le premier en France / Fit sentir dans les vers une juste cadence." ("Finally, Malherbe came, and was the first in France/To make us feel in verse a justified cadence.") [JG]

Saint-Michel.[32] He even received the anxious, but indeed disinterested, visits of Picasso, who was still called a master only by the poets.[33]

Van Dongen, Picasso's neighbor in Montmartre, seemed the most solitary then,[34] a loner quite similar to Edgar Poe's "Man of the Crowd," though more naive.[35]

Cézanne had just died.[36] He was not mourned. Major pieces of his estate were being transformed into knickknacks. But there was a distinct tendency, among those who were to become the future, to go further back than this master. Their works were astonishing at the Indépendants', Vollard's and Clovis Sagot's galleries, when they did not end up at the improbable merchant on the rue des Martyrs,[37] who grew wealthy by fleecing painters and renting out folding beds to the Medrano Circus performers.

---

[32]   Matisse moved into 19 quai Saint-Michel in 1899. [BGN]

[33]   Apollinaire, Max Jacob and Salmon. [JG]

[34]   Kees van Dongen (1877–1968) lived at the "Bateau Lavoir," a building with studios that looked like a wash boat, at 13 rue Ravignan, Montmartre, where Picasso lived from 1904–9. Van Dongen and Picasso both painted Picasso's mistress Fernande Olivier and exhibited in Daniel-Henry Kahnweiler's gallery at 28 rue Vignon. [BGN]

[35]   Edgar Allan Poe's "Man of the Crowd" was written in 1840. It tells the story of a *flaneur* who sits in a coffee shop looking out the window and then spontaneously decides to follow "a decrepit old man some sixty-five or seventy years of age" through the streets of London, seeking to infer some sense of the stranger's identity through his itinerary. [BGN]

[36]   Paul Cézanne died on October 23, 1906, during the Salon d'automne of that year. [BGN]

[37]   Le Père Soulié sold paintings in Montmartre in front of the Medrano Circus on the sidewalk of the rue des Martyrs in the middle of linens, quilts and other bedding. He bought Picasso's Blue Period paintings for very little. See André Salmon, *L'Air de la Butte*, Arcadia, 2004 repr., 176–177. [JG]

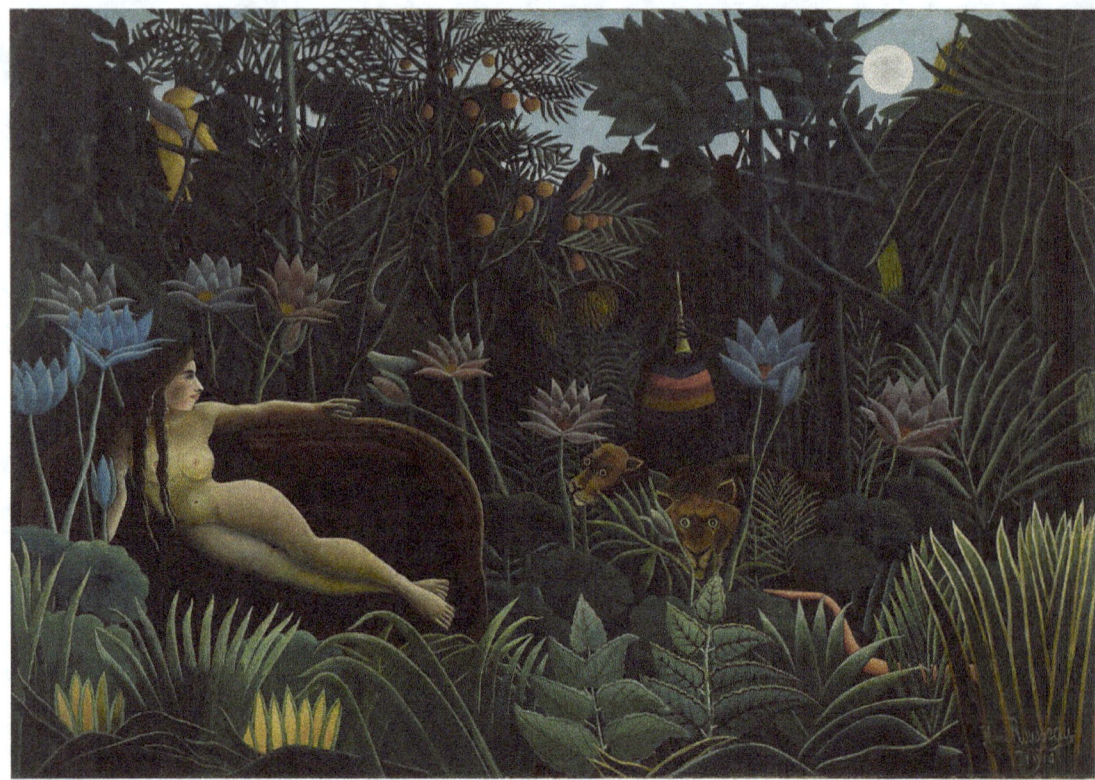

Figure 5. Henri Rousseau, *The Dream*, 1910
Museum of Modern Art, New York

It was Henri Rousseau, the customs officer painter, to whom the young artists gave the empire. His modest sovereignty especially favored the ambitions of the prince-electors. Finally, this election had the mark of a fine revolutionary act.[38]

---

[38] This "revolutionary act" literally took place during one memorable evening. At the end of 1908, Picasso bought a large portrait of the Douanier's first wife at Père Soulié's shop. This purchase inspired a parody to glorify Rousseau at a "banquet" held in Picasso's Bateau-Lavoir studio. Four accounts have been written by four of the guests who attended the "banquet": Maurice Raynal in the revue *Les Soirées de Paris*, n. 20, January 15, 1914; Fernande Olivier in her *Picasso and His Friends* (originally published in French as *Picasso et ses amis*, Paris: Stock, 1933); Gertrude Stein in the *Autobiography of Alice B. Toklas*, New York: Harcourt, Brace and Company, 1933; and Salmon in *Souvenirs sans fin*, Paris: Gallimard, 1956; reprinted in 2004. [JG]

The autodidact Henri Rousseau ingeniously challenged, in the name of all the Fauves, Luc-Olivier Merson and his academic peers as well as Besnard with the whole Société Nationale des Beaux-Arts.[39] Besides, le Douanier[40] deserved being noticed. Those who solidly established his renown were the least taken in, but they have fixed his destiny and they were well paid for it. Trade with Rousseau, that prodigiously intuitive man, was never without profit.

Certainly, if the Fauves had seriously believed in the necessity to name a Prince of Arts—like the people of letters[41]—their votes would probably go to Odilon Redon. But they needed a virgin ancestor, an American uncle, made rich with innumerable jewels confined in their matrix of rock and ore.

Mr. Uhde, in his clairvoyant monograph, wrote:

Rousseau, who knew nothing about the history of art, has attained in his body of work more than one zenith in painting. We were right, when standing in front of his large portraits, we called to mind the names Fouquet and Clouet, and in front of the smaller ones we remembered Holbein. There are pictures by him painted in the spirit of Brueghel, others reminiscent of Giotto, Taddeo Gaddi and Uccello. Others still make us think of Corot's first style, and some of his paintings of virgin forests are connected to the old art from Gobelins.[42]

---

[39] In 1890, the Société Nationale des Beaux-Arts separated from the Société des Artistes Français, which had taken over the organization of the annual Salon at the end of 1880, in order to create its own exhibition with less restrictive rules. Among the Société Nationale members were Ernest Meissonier, Pierre Puvis de Chavannes, Auguste Rodin, Alfred Stevens, Giovanni Boldini, John Singer Sargent, Eugène Carrière, Carolus-Duran, Alfred Sisley and Louis Anquetin. [BGN]

[40] This appellation refers to Rousseau who was stationed in a booth at the city gate in Montrouge in order to control the entry of certain taxable goods into Paris, thus earning him the nickname "le Douanier" ("the Customs Officer"). [JG]

[41] At the beginning of the twentieth century the election of a "Prince of Poets" was perpetuated in memory of Paul Verlaine (1844–1896), who was the first elected to that honor. See "Foreword" n. 16. [JG]

[42] Wilhelm Uhde, *Henri Rousseau*, Paris, Falguière, 1911. Founded in the fifteenth century in Paris, Gobelins was famous for manufacturing tapestries. [JG]

How could such a painter fail to gain the affection of artists who were nauseated by everything that was painted then, just as Arthur Rimbaud in 1870 was disgusted by the Romantic Baudelairian and Parnassian poetry.

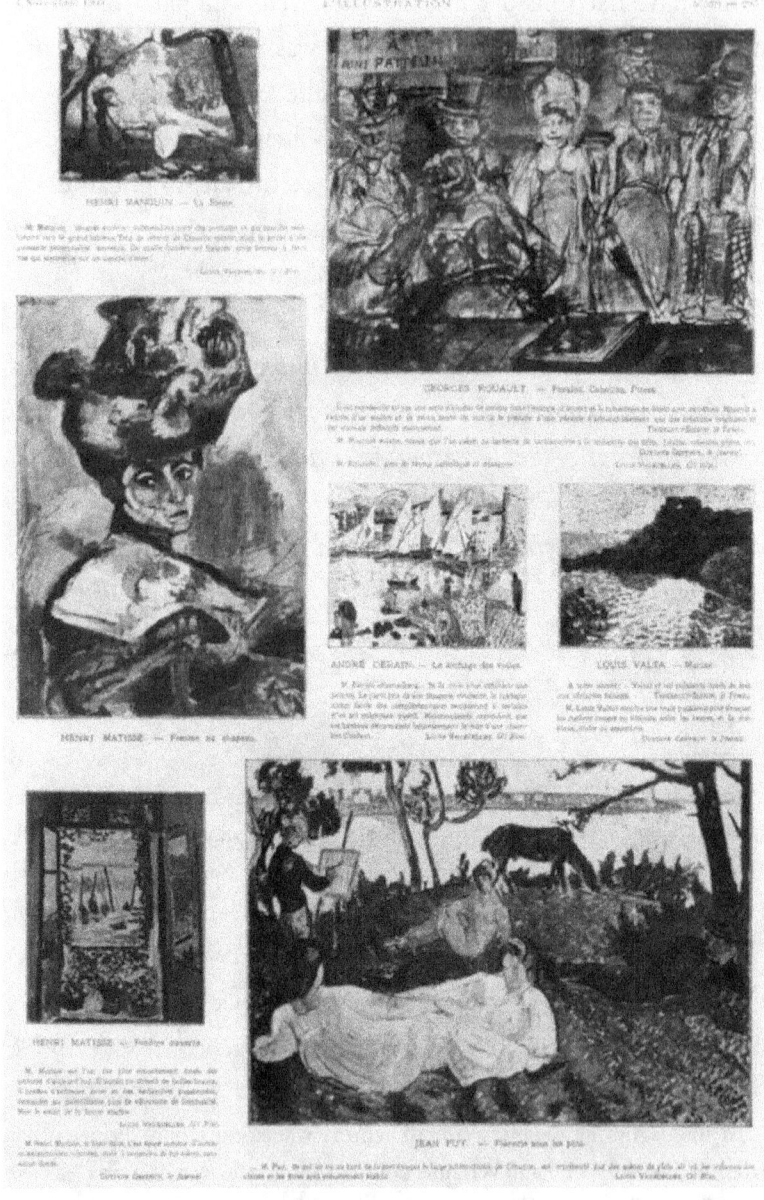

Figure 6. Fauves Exhibition at the Salon d'Automne, in *L'Illustration*, November 4, 1905

Thus, several artists were brought together, in a more or less occult manner (and many of them around this gentle old man from Montrouge[43]): Matisse, Picasso, Derain, Vlaminck, Marquet (always outside the mainstream and the first to leave the group), van Dongen, Othon Friesz, Georges Braque and Raoul Dufy.

Because they formed a group and this group was a new force, it was understood at the Indépendants' that they needed to be together in the same room. Hated by most, they appeared, nevertheless (and indeed justly so), as the saviors of that Society, exhausted before its thirtieth year.[44]

Old glories had passed to the Salon d'Automne, while others were no longer a draw. The then young artists (minus Picasso who never exhibited[45]) were about to insult a public who would pay to become upset!

From under the hill some young people looked up to these new gods. They begged, saying: "Hold your hand out to us!" and thought: "When we are on top, we will devour you."

Robert Delaunay, disgusted with little dots,[46] was discovering the Eiffel Tower, already used by the Douanier Rousseau; Miss Marie Laurencin was

---

[43] See note 40. Henri Rousseau, called le Douanier, was born in Laval on May 21, 1844. For Salmon and Picasso, both born in October 1881, he seemed to be an old man. Rousseau died in Paris on September 2, 1910, and was buried in a pauper's grave in Cimetière de Bagneux on September 4th. In March 1912, his remains were exhumed and transferred to an individual plot. Then in 1942, the Comité des amis d'Henri Rousseau reburied his remains in Jardin de la Perrine, near the municipal museum in Laval. Salmon served as treasurer on the committee (See "De Plaisance à l'Opéra," in Salmon's 1945 memoir, *L'Air de la Butte* [Paris: Arcadia, 2004 rep.], 116. Translated into English by Beth Gersh-Nešić and Jacqueline Gojard, in ATA ***Source,*** the online publication from the Literary Division, Spring 2011, 20–7). [BGN/JG]

[44] The Salon des Indépendants, launched by the Société des Artistes Indépendants, became an annual exhibition beginning in December 1884. This exhibition had no jury. [BGN] It benefited for a long time as a *succès de scandale*. [JG]

[45] Picasso refused to participate in the salons and preferred to exhibit in the galleries or to sell directly to the collectors. [JG]

[46] Salmon means here the pointillist style. [JG]

painting flowers with more quiet audacity than Matisse, and added grace to the Douanier's style. Her true personality, substantial but somewhat limited, was to awaken soon. Jean Metzinger suffered from devoting himself to an art requiring such a meager expenditure of intelligence. The road to salvation grew wider. But who should be followed: Matisse or Picasso?

Oh, glory days!

If they speculated feverishly (not without a lot of gaiety at Picasso's studio and infinitely less playfulness at Matisse's), they worked even more—each in a hurry to create a work for the battle.

In total ignorance of their mutual destinies, the painters still paid homage to each other, offering up characteristic studies considered by the givers gestures of collegiality.

Those small gifts did not contribute very much to sustaining a good friendship. One *Portrait of a Young Girl* was subjected to the most ridiculous insults by its owner and his guests.[47]

The immediately interested were not the only ones to practice "diplomatic courtesy." Some painters from the preceding generation, less favorably

---

[47]   This is a reference to the exchange of paintings between Picasso and Matisse that took place in 1907. Picasso gave Matisse *Pitcher, Bowl and Lemon,* now in the Fondation Beyeler, Basel, and Matisse gave Picasso *Portrait of Marguerite,* now in the Musée Picasso, Paris. In *Souvenirs sans fin* (Paris: Gallimard, 1955, rep. 2004, 198), Salmon describes how Picasso and his guests would aim suction arrows at the portrait along with such remarks as "Pan! in the eye of Marguerite!" and "Right on the cheek!" In Gertrude Stein's *The Autobiography of Alice B. Toklas* (in the 1961 reprint on page 64), Stein wrote: "They exchanged pictures as was the habit in those days. Each painter chose the one of the other one that presumably interested him the most. Matisse and Picasso chose each one of the other one the pictures that were undoubtedly the least interesting either of them had done. Later each one used it as an example, the picture he had chosen, of the weaknesses of the other one. Very evidently in the two pictures chosen the strong qualities of each painter were not much in evidence." Pierre Daix recorded his conversation with Picasso on Matisse's painting: "'Doesn't that remind you of something?' [Picasso asked.] Perhaps my eyes followed his as we looked at the canvas [*Portrait of Marguerite*]. 'Her nose is sideways, like the noses of the *Demoiselles*?' [Picasso] laughed, like someone who had made a successful point." [BGN]

situated than a Bonnard, a Vuillard, or a Desvallières,[48] yearned to join the Fauve contingent.

We saw them then, seniors and juniors, unfailingly attracted to the camp of the damned—dreading anemia and stuffing themselves on rich food!

The foreigners in Paris followed the movement without nobility, plagiarizing with ease, knowing nothing about the anxieties of the young masters, satisfied with their barbarian taste, which they believed was a break with tradition, and above all, driven by a confident instinct for the art-lover's next appetite.

Hermann-Paul, a delicate spirit and a painter who seemed out of breath, foresaw the possibility of rejuvenating himself through Fauvism.[49] As early as the Salon of 1906, the Fauves were a force.

It is important to emphasize the diversity of those artists, not many of whom remain today faithful to the belief of that time.

We can no longer study the work of Marquet. Already glory has crowned him. He no longer belongs to us.

On the other hand, if we take pains to define the role of the illustrious Henri Matisse—that is because those who stem more or less directly from this painter, or march alongside him, are still in the midst of the struggle, armed by him.

⚬✖⚬

We knew of literary cases during the Symbolist period that were somewhat similar to that of Henri Matisse. Leaders came along authorizing wonderful boldness. Others had the strength and delight of achieving it.

From 1895–1899,[50] Henri Matisse painted conscientiously and not without vigor. He was a serious student of Gustave Moreau, who consulted

---

[48] Artist Georges-Olivier Desvallières (1861–1950) was born and died in Paris. [BGN]

[49] René-Georges Hermann-Paul (1874–1940), a painter who was close to the Nabis, is known today mostly for his engravings, caricatures and illustrations. [JG]

[50] Henri Matisse (1869–1954) studied with Gustave Moreau (born in Paris in 1826) from 1892 until the master's death in 1898. Albert Marquet (1875–1947) joined the studio in 1893. [BGN]

the Realists. At the dawn of the twentieth century, he seemed anxious and, piercing the academic screen, made a comforting appeal to light—not as a successor of the Impressionists, who were only curious about an instant of light.

All of a sudden, an important and violent revolution took place: Fauvism was invented. Others would explore with Henri Matisse, breaking with ancient laws; several, who were already searching, felt comforted by his audacity and followed him.

Henri Matisse, who wanted the greatest amount of light, while repudiating artificial light, discovered only color, and that discovery was bound to enslave him. Nevertheless, his best still-life paintings and somewhat pleasant pictures of flowers date from this period.

Then came the landscapes from Collioure, the celebrated *Woman with Green Eyes*,[51] and those nudes with an intentional, always arbitrary drawing, the only ones, among his works, which bear witness to a logical effort in order to reach a style. Step by step Henri Matisse has contradicted himself, and in that way he is the most incoherent of modern artists.

His true gifts are the gifts of skill, flexibility, rapid assimilation, and limited but quickly acquired knowledge—feminine gifts. The more he acquires facility, the more color triumphs over the drawing—which finally no longer counts. His drawing is summary, reduced to the latest discoveries that absorb the essential. In addition, the figures are multiples of three or four characters tirelessly repeated, of which *Man with a Violin* is an example.[52]

Henri Matisse's taste was praised a lot. It is undeniable, but of an inferior quality, the taste of a milliner; his love of color is the equivalent to the love of drapery.

---

[51] *Girl with Green Eyes*, autumn-winter 1908, painted at the Hôtel Biron, now in the collection of the San Francisco Museum of Modern Art. [BGN]

[52] This title may refer to *Music*, 1909–10, which was made for Sergei Shchukin (The Hermitage Museum, Saint Petersburg) or the study for *Music*, 1907, which belonged to Gertrude Stein (Museum of Modern Art, New York). Both have a violinist standing on the extreme left side. [BGN]

So, this master who reigned over an academy was not the leader. In truth, he was only the teacher. Henri Matisse's lessons would not be sought out except by those minor artists sent to Paris from abroad. Whereas young painters in Germany translate Matisse, like Berlin vaudevillians translate our playwrights, the French salons are less and less cluttered with Moscovite and Scandinavian *matisseries*.[53]

What was fortunate and of merit in the work of the first Fauve—and which came from Odilon Redon—was absorbed by the painters who are the most diverse and the most alien to his immediate preoccupations.

Such were all Henri Matisse's endeavors. Along with Picasso and Derain, he interrogated barbarian idol-makers, perhaps he even found out about them before Picasso.[54] The lesson of the Polynesian, Dahomeyan and Sudanese artists was listened to. Then we forgot Henri Matisse, a victim of his impatience to achieve his own virtuosity, without delay.

This painter who, in spite of everything, somehow seems to be a great painter (in the way that some great poets are not pure poets) is from now on an isolated person.

Othon Friesz, who followed him more closely, was the first to keep his distance. All is nihilism in the work of Henri Matisse; it does not go anywhere. It is sterile, although it should not be ignored.

---

[53] Matisse opened a school in 1908 at 56 rue de Sèvres. Among his students were the German Hans Purrmann and the Americans Sarah Stein (wife of Michael Stein, sister-in-law of Gertrude Stein) and Patrick Henry Bruce. [BNG]

The word "matisseries" was created by Salmon as a play on the word "pâtisseries" (pastry) to make fun of Matisse's disciples who thought that they could make a painting like one makes a cake, with a mold. [JG]

[54] According to Matisse in a 1941 interview with Pierre Courthion, the artist came by Gertrude Stein's one day in 1906 with a nineteenth-century Vili sculpture from the Congo. Picasso was there and admired it (Jack Flam, "Matisse and the Fauves," in *"Primitivism" in the 20th Century* [New York: The Museum of Modern Art, 1984], 216–217, 238, n. 47; Henri Matisse, "Matisse Speaks," statements to E. Teriade, *Art News Annual*, 21, New York, 1952). [BGN]

We have to think about it, not so much because of the enthusiasm it provoked for an instant, but on account of the definitive date it marks in the history of painting.

Henri Matisse and Picasso, whose careers are no longer predictable, were destined to give the signal to a paroxysm of talents which will live longer in our memory than the Romantic revolution.

The case of André Derain is somewhat singular. He lives outside the mainstream of contemporary painting, and I am not sure that his extended retirement does not carry with it some dangers.[55]

We will see in the course of the next chapter the role this artist played in the history of Cubism (though no Cubist can claim him as a member of his family).

It is impossible to devote an important study to the work of an artist who has refused to exhibit any work for the last four years.

If, on the other hand, we had the time to examine the role of André Derain as a revealer of truths, we would need to devote quite an extensive monograph to him, at least as long as this book.

Along with Matisse and Picasso, he compelled his generation to recall the Gauguin's words: "It seems that Europe is unaware that quite an advanced decorative art existed among the Maoris of New Zealand and the Marquesas."[56]

---

[55] Early in his career, André Derain (1880–1954) was close with Vlaminck, Picasso, Braque, Salmon, Max Jacob and Guillaume Apollinaire. In October 1907, Picasso introduced Derain to the mathematician Maurice Princet's wife Alice. Derain married Alice in 1908. Salmon's reference to a "retirement" may be Derain's exclusive arrangement with Daniel-Henry Kahnweiler, who began showing Derain's work in 1909. By 1910, Derain only exhibited at Kahnweiler's gallery and not at the salons. In 1908, Derain had destroyed a large number of his early works (Jane Lee, *Derain* [New York: Universe/Oxford: Phaidon, 1990], 28–29). [BGN]

[56] In Paul Gauguin, *The Writings of a Savage*, edited by Daniel Guérin and translated by Eléonor Levieux (New York: Viking Press, 1974), 279: "People in Europe do not seem to realize that both the Maoris of New Zealand and the Marquesans had evolved a very advanced type of decorative art. Mr. Know-it-all-Critic is wrong when he dismisses it all as 'Papuan art'!" [BGN]

Those words were commented on by Charles Morice (a critic whose reputation will survive for having brought attention to Gauguin, Carrière, Rodin, as he already had called attention to Tristan Corbière and—why not mention—Verlaine[57]) with such accuracy: "This art is the true art. It is the one that connects Mexico to Egypt; Cambodians to the Gothics; archaic Greeks to the Italian, Flemish and French Primitives, and the Japanese and the Chinese; and Giotto to Puvis de Chavannes. It is the art that makes the unity of races and centuries varied and changeless; the art that is the human expression of nature. It is ancient art."

An admirable affirmation. However, Charles Morice wrote that in 1910, and André Derain was already aware of it two years prior to that.

Derain did more. He can be credited, for the most part, with having restored the glory of El Greco, who for many was still "The Lunatic."[58]

André Derain borrowed from him what an original artist can faithfully borrow from the masters. From this period come the admirable landscapes (which one might call pre-Cubist), the elements of which stem from El Greco's *View of Toledo*.[59]

These same elements, after a good deal of foolishness (perhaps necessary, and in any event inevitable), nourish today the works of the most happily liberated Cubists.

We hope that the next lesson André Derain will offer us might be as fruitful—when it pleases him to end his retirement and our deprivation.

---

[57] Gauguin entrusted the format of *Noa Noa* to his friend Charles Morice (1860–1919), a Symbolist writer, poet and essayist, who acted as his agent with his dealer Ambroise Vollard. Morice was also a friend of the poets. He made Tristan Corbière, the author of *Les Amours jaunes* (1873), widely known. Paul Verlaine dedicated his celebrated "Art poétique" to him. [JG]

[58] For a long time, El Greco was considered a mystical, unbalanced—even half-crazy—painter. His works were rediscovered in France at the beginning of the twentieth century. Picasso's *Burial of Casagemas* (1901) was inspired by El Greco's *Burial of Count Orgaz* (1586). [JG]

[59] An example from this period would be Derain's *Landscape at Cadaqués*, 1910, Národni Galerie, Prague. [BGN]

It doesn't matter if you think Jean Puy is an Impressionist, when in fact he isn't. Anyone who paints in front of nature can sometimes indeed encounter these masters of Neo-Realism without owing them anything.

Jean Puy is a painter of great sincerity; taking pains not to ignore anything that has to do with his craft, he wisely protects himself from old formulas, and he has that wisdom—the rarest of all—not to create any new ones.

The great value of Jean Puy—the least explosive, perhaps, but the most personal, to be sure—is in invention. Modern artists have for the last few years strangely limited, not to say altered, the sense of the word composition.

The Cubists' reaction has been the least deniable, which is not always—and not for everyone—possible to follow, nor should it be desirable.

Since Cézanne and Gauguin, how many (among those who do not exhibit foolish anecdotal works at the Salon des Artistes Français) still deign to compose a picture?

Jean Puy has the courage to dare as far as fantasy. But his fantasy is not extreme.

One of the most likable canvases by Puy, conceived in the course of the last few years, has this simple title: *Composition*. Is it intentional?

In the foreground are two young girls in bright dresses and behind them the painter stands at his easel. At his feet lies the nude model. Under a tree, a sailor takes his siesta. The sea fills the whole background of the canvas.[60]

Jean Puy would not let his imagination go beyond that. But isn't it enough if the artist feeds his fantasy with the same reasons that account for his effort?

An inventor of limited invention, he has no picturesque resources but within himself. However, he steers his most ordinary gestures toward the

---

[60] Jean Puy (1876–1960), *Lounging under the Pine Trees* (*Flânerie sous les pins*), 1905, Musée Paul Dini, Villefranche-sur-Sâone. This painting appears in the often-reproduced newspaper review of the Salon d'automne in *L'Illustration*, November 4, 1905, which shows works from the notorious "cage aux Fauves" (John Elderfield, *Fauvism: The "Wild Beasts" and Its Affinities* [New York: The Museum of Modern Art, 1976], 44). [BGN]

sublime; and his gesture is that of the painter tempted by beauty: the nudity of women, the innocence of merry children, and the abundance of the French landscape.

Jean Puy can be placed among the Fauves only for historic reasons, and because he was baptized a Fauve, despite himself. Henceforth famous, he could hardly be included in a book such as this one a year from now.

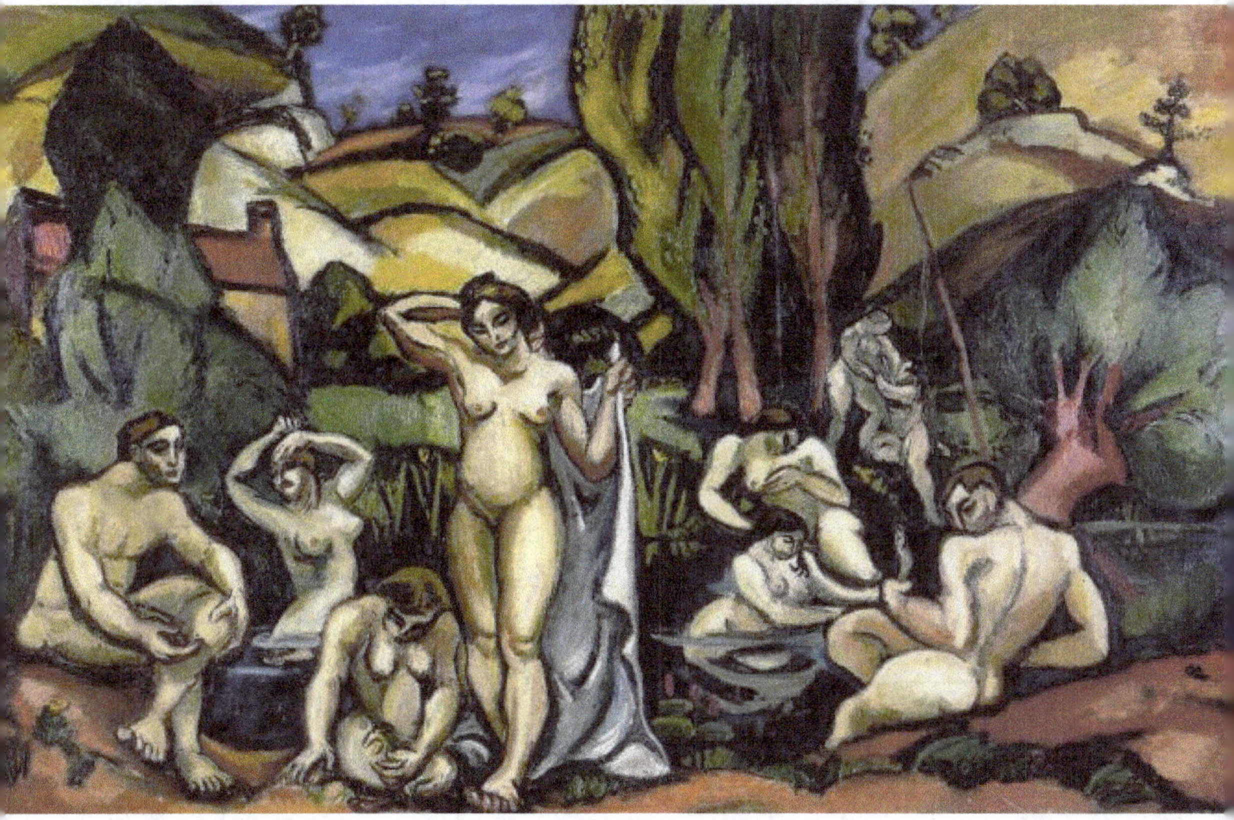

Figure 7. Othon Friesz, *The Bathers of Andelys*, 1908, Musée du Petit Palais, Geneva

Today, Othon Friesz remains the lone representative of an art whose limits he fixed ten years ago. But others, who had not enough sensitivity to follow him, owe him a considerable debt.

Striving with the happiest intelligence to provoke a rebirth of composition, Othon Friesz finally heard Poussin's lesson in order to make it clearer.

Now, Nicolas Poussin is an excellent headmaster for someone who wants to paint nature, since his vision is the most perfectly French vision of landscape. "In Rome, Nicolas Poussin would see the Andelys," said a commentator.[61]

The Normand Othon Friesz would have been quite capable of seeing the Andelys in Tahiti, because, along with two or three others, he knew how to obtain from Gauguin the only profitable lesson, the consequence of which is not the meager discovery of a quasi-fairground exoticism but the broadening of scenery toward the universal through the honesty of drawing and the purification of planes.

Like Nicolas Poussin, Othon Friesz wanted to create a "historic landscape," and through Poussin, he joins Gauguin (recently deceased)[62] since the great French Roman and the master from Tahiti have crudely interpreted the gestures of young maidens bathing a child in the Tiber or two guys from Pont-Aven fighting in the Forest of Love in order to paint, respectively, *Moses Saved in the Water* and *Jacob Wrestling with the Angel* (Gauguin, 1888).[63]

Now, Othon Friesz wanted to attain the perfect innocence of sentiment. The beautiful interpretations by Gauguin in the Marquesas Islands—that

---

[61] Nicolas Poussin was born in Les Andelys, near Rouen, in June 1594. He spent the greater part of his life in Rome where he died in 1665. His landscapes derive from an interior vision and the penchant for construction. He invented the use of "settings"—arbitrary architectural elements that structure the painting and that Friesz reprised. [JG]

[62] Paul Gauguin, born on June 7, 1848, died May 8, 1903, on Atuona, island of Hiva Oa, the Marquesas Islands. [BGN]

[63] Nicolas Poussin, *The Finding of Moses*, c. 1627–28, Musée du Louvre. [BGN] Paul Gauguin, *The Vision after the Sermon: Jacob Wrestling with the Angel*, 1888, National Gallery of Scotland, Edinburgh. [BGN]

poetry proceeding from uncertain and eternal myths—were to give him more satisfaction than the antique or sacred themes of Poussin.

Therefore, he put nudes in a virgin landscape that he discovered in Cassis[64] without crossing the seas. But, like his great ancestor, he remembered the Andelys under the Mediterranean blue sky.

Othon Friesz was counted among the Fauves by hasty critics because, anxious to express the movement, he resorted like them to deformation. His research was not always fortunate. He rarely has a feeling for repose, and his nudes can only satisfy us if the muscles in motion give the work its balance. Too often when Friesz paints a woman sleeping, he falsifies the attitude of his sleeper with an artificial and irrational play of muscles.

Upon returning to his native Normandy,[65] Othon Friesz came into his own by studying sites and monuments from Rouen to the Andelys. His *Rouen Cathedral* would definitively orient Robert Delaunay.[66] And the most skillful foreigners trivialized the beautiful harmony of graduated tones in his famous *Study at the Foot of the Cliff* that was so new at the time.

Like Nicolas Poussin, he embellished his landscapes with architectural elements, and these "settings," adopted by others, were to be the first stones of the Cubist temple.

---

[64] A little port near Marseille, where Friesz painted his famous *Fisherman* (1909). [JG]

[65] Émile Othon Friesz (1879–1949) was born in Le Havre, like his friend Raoul Dufy (1877–1953). [JG]

[66] Friesz painted *Roofs and Rouen Cathedral* in 1908 (now in the Hermitage Museum in St. Petersburg). Robert Delaunay (1885–1941) was influenced by the Fauves before becoming the leader of the Orphist movement with its "simultaneous contrasts." The composition in his *Factory in Chaville* (1909) is somewhat reminiscent of Friesz's *Cathedral*. [JG].

That already says a lot about the influence of this artist, who was not the head of a school, and yet from whom several (who no longer remember) have profited.[67]

Later, concerned about picturesque realism, Othon Friesz resorted occasionally to popular art. His celebrated *Fisherman* is an interpretation of typical images, but, frankly speaking, he revives him in front of the sea; and the beautiful frigate (so servilely adopted by several artists) that he placed in several corners of his seascape compositions, is the same frigate with the heavy sails that decorates the clay pipe of all the fishermen from the Channel.

It was enough for artists, who were still uncertain, to develop a taste for the images. Friesz should not be held too fully responsible for that, since these artists, mistaken about his real intentions, sometimes went so far as to make the painting appear like a print.

Since then, Othon Friesz has asserted himself through his powerful circus scenes and Portuguese landscapes in which he has shown his purest gifts as a constructor and a colorist.

We would have nothing to say about Dufy (whose work as a painter is not very substantial), if he were not the architect of a great misunderstanding.

As an engraver, he was the first to be concerned with restoring the loss of elegance in a popular art that had only been awkwardly parodied in some poetic publications during the Symbolist period.

---

[67] Salmon may be referring to the summer of 1907, when Friesz and Braque painted together in La Ciotat, departing from Paris sometime after the opening of the Cézanne exhibition at Berheim-Jeune gallery on June 17. Derain, who was staying in Cassis, wrote to Vlaminck, "Their idea is young and to them seems new; they'll get over it." (William Rubin, *Picasso and Braque: Pioneering Cubism* [New York: The Museum of Modern Art, 1989], 344). This summer for these Fauve artists was dominated by Cézannism, the prelude to Cubism (Beth Gersh-Nešić, "Cézannisme and Cézannismes: Examining the Literature on Cubism," paper given at the Mediterranean Studies Association conference, May 2001, Aix-en-Provence). See also William Rubin, "Cézannisme and the Beginnings of Cubism," in *Cézanne: The Late Work*, exhibition catalogue (New York: The Museum of Modern Art, 1977), 151–202. [BGN]

In fact, he knew how to re-create this art with all its authentic naivity, and he produced, without doubt, the masterpiece of modern original engraving: *Orpheus' Procession.*[68]

Then, as if he were ashamed of no longer being a painter, Dufy again took up his brushes. With dryness, and also a naivety that was no longer genuine, he painted perfunctory little figures in some sparse landscapes. It was scarcely imagery, an art far inferior to that of the old masters from Strasbourg or Mulhouse—wallpaper, an art beneath the great engraver that was Dufy.

His example was to be followed. More definitively than Friesz, he had cluttered modern painting with shoddy art for a long time to come.

His panegyrists praise him for having discovered everything: Cubism would not exist without him. That is to go far afield.[69] He himself has singularly limited his role, and today Dufy gives his full attention only to the study of pure decoration[70] from which one should expect a lot.

Georges Rouault continues Daumier, but as a student of Gustave Moreau,[71] who witnessed the great pictorial revolutions after Impressionism.

---

[68] Raoul Dufy produced woodcuts to illustrate Guillaume Apollinaire's poems in *Le Bestiaire, ou Cortège d'Orphée*, Paris: Deplanche, 1911. [BGN]

[69] Dufy joined Braque in L'Estaque during the summer of 1908 (Rubin, *Picasso and Braque*, 353). Allegedly, Matisse described Braque's L'Estaque paintings as only little "cubes." See "Anecdotal History of Cubism." [BNG]

[70] In 1911–1912, Dufy teamed up with Paul Poiret and worked for the Lyonnais silk company Bianchini-Ferrier. He would find his style and produce his best works after World War I. Salmon called attention to his quality in *L'Art vivant* (Crès, 1920). [JG]

[71] Georges Rouault (1871–1958), alongside Matisse and Marquet, studied with Gustave Moreau from 1892 (the first year that the master had been assigned an École des Beaux-Arts class) to 1898, when Moreau died. [BGN]

The choice of clownish models is not always about producing irony, and we cannot say that Georges Rouault enjoys jingling the bells of the mournful caricature.[72]

He has a powerful vision of life, corresponding to a very deep sensitivity. Georges Rouault simply contents himself with models that his period offers him. If they are often odious, it is because the artist is a painter of characters and a rather ingenuous man, so that his brush translates with a sort of sacred terror the villainy of souls. However, this preoccupation is secondary for Rouault, who is above all interested in physical substance, from shape to color. He is a Realist who always sees broadly and often accurately.

His judges are shameful, his bourgeois infamous, and his girls exhale the pestilence of vulgar vice. But how touching are those clowns, as colorful as their crazy speech, those disjointed Pierrots, those nude women (mere animals), and those peasants—bound to the clay[73] more than others, because their faces are the very color of rich tillage.

The drawing and the arrangement of subjects belong particularly to Rouault, who, as a colorist, only developed to the utmost the lessons of Gustave Moreau. Perhaps, Rouault is the only artist of our time who has indeed known how to translate a true feeling from the popular soul.

Van Dongen owes the brutality of his form to the violence of his passions. He began a little less than fifteen years ago with some libertarian[74] drawings. He arrived here straight from his native Holland. He was poor and sensual.

In the studio of a mutual friend, as I was leafing through a magazine enhanced by a photograph of Miss. M. revealing the charm of a supple leg

---

[72] From Charles Baudelaire's "The Death of Artists" (*Les Fleurs du Mal*, 1867): "Combien de fois faut-il secouer mes grelots, / Et baiser ton front bas, morne caricature?": "How often must I jingle my bells/And kiss your lowly brow, mournful Caricature." [JG]

[73] In French, the word *argile* which Salmon uses here is loaded with significant meaning. Salmon refers to the rich earth used by potters and sculptors, which God himself used to create the first man. He is sensitive to the thick impasto Rouault applies to his canvases and their profoundly religious character. [JG]

[74] Salmon chose the word *libertaire* rather than *libertin*, deliberately characterizing van Dongen's Fauvism as anarchic instead of sexually explicit. [BGN]

between the arabesques of a skimpy crinoline, van Dongen said to me: "Are you too a glutton for these things?"

As a libertarian,[74] he envied the middle-class man capable of providing himself with, as a modern poet would say, a scattered harem. As a foreigner, he was astonished, like all common tourists lacking in refinement, by the vulgar but dazzling entertainment at a Moulin-Rouge or a Monico.[75] We must also admit that the great ghost of the tragic monster, the genius puppet, the painful gentleman Henri de Toulouse-Lautrec, still visited painters: Picasso himself had barely escaped his grip.

Thus, van Dongen celebrated frilly lewdness. He was the painter of commercial boudoirs, pay toilets, brothels, can-can balls, the turned-up skirt, and the garter.

But the suggestive filth of current raunchy expressions repulsed this libertarian. Through violence, he got away from a too obvious triteness. Only his astonishment is of a somewhat vulgar quality. What one must value in van Dongen is the personal character of his painting, even more than that of his drawing.

A painter of easy girls, he learned from his models the art of painting and confused the artist's box of colors with the prostitute's box of makeup—a fertile and picturesque error. Logical, and in his way an advocate of direct action,[76] he gave to his figures inhumanly large eyes, because courtesans make their eyes bigger with black, kohl and blue. All the early work of van Dongen shows the formidable appetite of a sensual proletarian, hungry for bourgeois meat.

Having attained great notoriety and become almost rich, here is the very modern Dutchman, a bourgeois in his turn. From the comrade of yesterday,

---

[75] The can-can was danced at the Moulin-Rouge and the pan-pan was danced at the Monico, two famous cabarets in the hot Pigalle district in Paris. Gino Severini's *Dancing the "Pan-Pan" at the Monico*, 1909–11, exhibited in Galerie Bernheim-Jeune's February 1912 Futurist exhibition (today in the permanent collection of the National Museum of Modern Art, Centre Pompidou, in Paris) interprets the gyrating crowd. [JG]

[76] The principal of "direct action" was one of the fundamental concepts of anarchist ideology. [JG]

he has retained his cynicism, but he is becoming more refined. His desire is less vast because he can possess; he embraces with more delicacy adulterated beauty, which is dear to him. He even experienced an instant of snobbism, and a certain Salon d'Automne exhibited him as a worldly painter, a sufficiently correct competitor to worry Messrs. François Flameng and Boldini.[77]

But van Dongen rejuvenates himself through surprise because it is his fate to wonder. A trip to Morocco restored his initial innocence. He remains brutal and naïve—nearly nothing in the art of composition—the painter of the most beautiful girls whose profession consists in revealing as much as possible of their physical splendor. Like them, he does not turn up his nose at aphrodisiac artifice, and colors his nudes in pink tones like sunsets, with golden kohl like secret folds, and with the blue of weary mornings. He likes, more than live gardens, crazy hats that are as beautiful as fairy-tale groves, sumptuous stockings and all the trappings of gallantry.

Van Dongen is, in sum, a candid Fleming with an extraordinarily sincere eye, who took the spectacles of a complicated and rigorously arranged debaucher for one of the most evident signs of a civilization going beyond what he had ever thought possible.

Pierre Girieud,[78] an artist of good breeding and remarkably gifted, missed being the Gustave Moreau of Fauvism. The inclination of his imagination subjected him to this danger. He knew, in time, to take up the study of the old Italian masters again, and if he does not revive the greatest ones, he often

---

[77] François Flameng, son of the engraver Léopold Flameng (1831–1911), studied with Alexandre Cabanel, Edmond Hédouin (1820–1889) and Jean-Paul Laurens (1838–1921). He was well known for his fashionable portraits and history paintings, such as his mural *Music* in the Salon des Arts of the Hôtel de Ville, Paris. Giovanni Boldini was a society portraitist. Both mixed academic realism with painterly expression in the clothing, furniture and background. [BGN]

[78] Pierre Paul Girieud (1876–1948) studied with Jules Monge (1855–1934), a student of Cabanel's. [BGN]

reminds us of Palma il Vecchio, who equally liked to paint Holy Families, Dianas, Venuses and Marsyases.

As it happened to certain Symbolist poets, purifying a phantasmagoric imagination through their implementation of rejuvenated eternal myths, Pierre Girieud's qualities as an allegorical painter were soaked in antique sources.

He was linked to the Fauves by what first united them all: color.

Pierre Girieud created for himself a palette no less violent than that of a van Dongen or a Henri Matisse, which belonged to him alone by virtue of a certain choice of yellows, blues, and greens punctuated with vermilion. But on the canvas, he knew how to tone down the harmony by degrees through the distribution of colors. Some of his violently garish first works are already very similar to distempered paintings.

Pierre Girieud was still a Fauve at the beginning of his career, due to the barbarity of his imagination—and of the worst kind. The products of his fantasy too often bore the signature of the Montmartroise chimera's paw: In his stained-glass projects and his pictures at that time, almost all of which seem to be stained-glass projects, green toads with red eyes (loved by Jean Lorrain[79]) and golden spiders abound. A trip to Italy brought about a healthy moderation. Pierre Girieud called forth his background, loathing his barbarian devotions, and refining in such a manner that we may see him a little like a classically inspired decadent. Thus, he still hasn't returned to the grand tradition. Freer than those two contemporaries, he belongs to the same family as Alexandre Séon and Ary Renan.[80] In fact, he is not completely foreign to

---

[79] Jean Lorrain (1855–1906), pseudonym of Paul Duval, was a journalist and novelist with a Decadent flavor. [BGN]

[80] Alexandre Séon (1855–1917) and Ary Renan (1858–1916) were Symbolist painters. Ary Renan, son of the renowned historian Ernest Renan (1823–1892), also wrote art criticism. [BGN]

Miss Hélène Dufau.[81] And all of that allows us to legitimately say that he missed being our Gustave Moreau.

Since he formed himself and developed among us, the Dutchman Verhoeven has to be ranked among the important figures of young French painting (for the same reason as his compatriot van Dongen and several others). At the moment, Verhoeven remains perfectly Fauve. He even has evolved a lot less than Henri Matisse. His inspiration comes from India and the Far East.

His models are Indian dancing women. Their apparent immobility comes only from capturing a brief instant of the most vertiginous of the dances. Isn't that all the frozen splendor of Nirvana?

The tormented and frenetic universe contemplated from a unique angle that allows us to catch a glimpse of it, as perfectly immobile.

But from this agitation there remains a rending of the most hieratic attitude. In Verhoeven's work, lines and color masses are torn and mangled—reduced to bundles of fibers. Without doubt, one has to see in this manner the latest application of Neo-Impressionist doctrines.

However, movement—which we must acknowledge exists in the works of Seurat, Cross, Signac and Luce—is always absent from the work of Verhoeven.

He does not compose. There is torpor and laziness in his creations. His arbitrarily isolated figures suffer from being extracted from the group that they denote.

---

[81] Clémentine-Hélène Dufau (1869–1937) was a fashionable artist at the time of this publication. She painted murals in the writer Edmond Rostand's luxurious Villa Arnaga, located in the Basque Country and unfortunately fell in love with his son Maurice Rostand, an intimate friend of Marcel Proust's. Forgotten for a long time, she has recently been rediscovered. Her beautiful self-portrait is on display in the Musée d'Orsay in Paris, and one can visit the Villa Arnaga, which became the Musée Edmond Rostand. [JG]

Alcide Le Beau admires the extreme skills of some masters from the empire of the Rising Sun. And yet, since he is a modern European, pictorial chaos seduces him. Thus, he arrives at a disconcerting (at first) mixture of finish, of meticulous detail and of confusion.

One could say that certain canvases, such as the river landscapes, among his best, would reflect an accomplished disorder.

However, Alcide Le Beau is becoming, from one day to the next, more personal; his skill is no less great and is losing what was irritating about it.

Heir to Cézanne twice removed, while Alcide Le Beau keeps Matisse's glasses on his nose, his eyes slowly succeed in boring through them.

The Manguin[82] drawing is often arbitrary; it is a mixture (sometimes savory) of foreign boldness and academicism. In his best days he joins, in turn, Charles Guérin and Jean Puy.

We can believe that Manguin wanted to reconcile everyone. As a result, he bypasses them all, and he belongs no more at the National Salon than at the Indépendants. But at the Artistes Français, he would seem a terrible man.

However, this artist knows a lot. He is skillful, too skillful; his composition—not a very personal one—lacks neither balance nor charm in a certain calculated abandon. Too many concessions lead sometimes to incoherence despite an initial gift.

The gravest reproach that one can make to this painter, who has the great ambitions of a colorist, is his lack of certainty in taste (his crude landscapes testify to that), which is however far, quite far, from being an absence of taste.

---

[82] In contradistinction to Jan Verhoeven (1870–1941) and Alcide Le Beau (1873–1943), Henri Manguin (1874–1949) is considered today one of the principal Fauves. Numerous books are written about him, and he benefited from a wonderful retrospective in the Musée de L'Annonciade in Saint-Tropez, in 2011. [JG] And during the summer of 2015, a retrospective at the Musée Bonnard in Le Cannet, Côte d'Azur. [BGN]

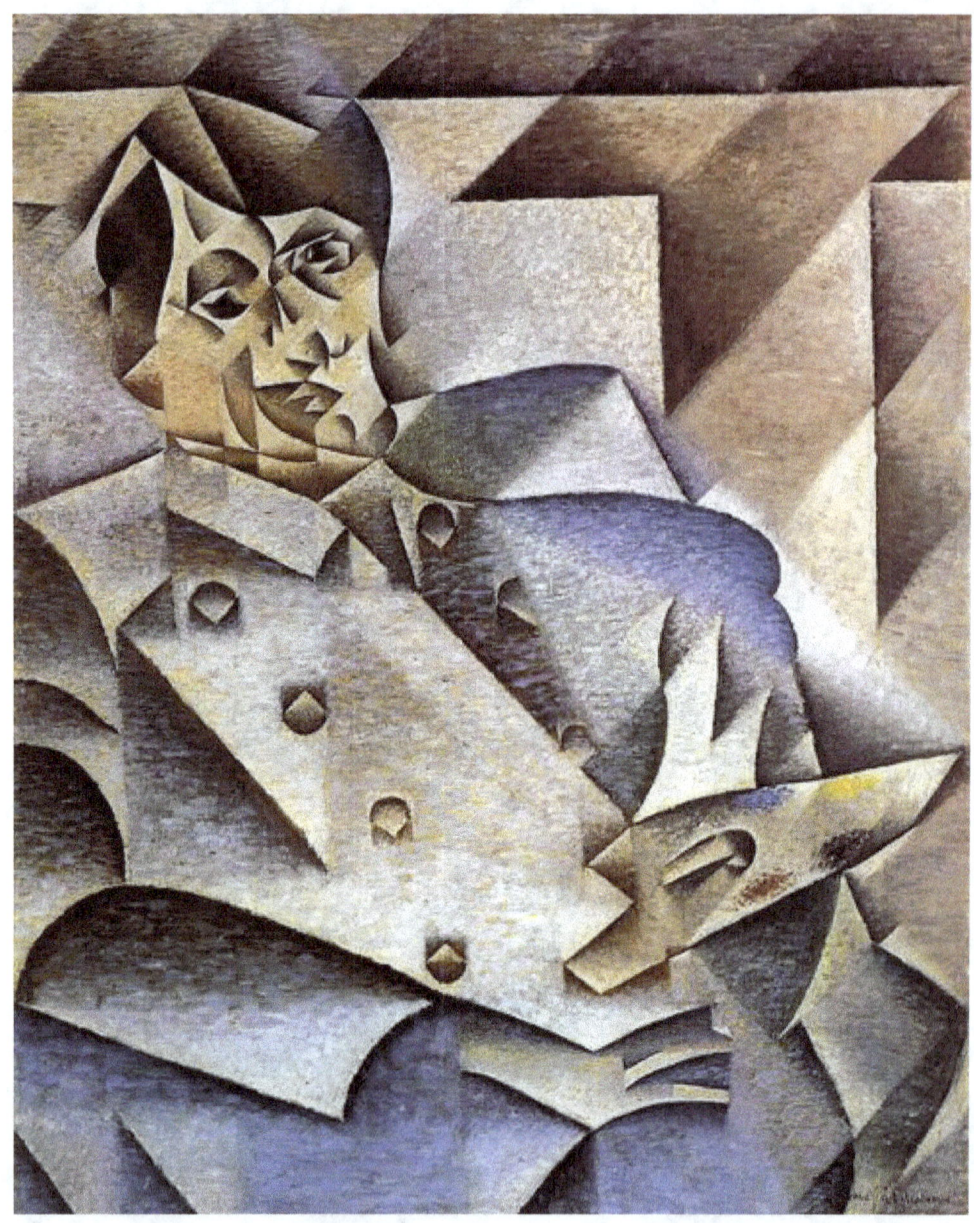

Figure 8. Juan Gris, *Portrait of Pablo Picasso*, 1912,
Art Institute of Chicago

2

An Anecdotal History of Cubism

At the time, Picasso was leading a wonderful life. His uninhibited genius had never blossomed more radiantly.

From El Greco to Toulouse-Lautrec, he had consulted masters worthy of reigning over disturbed souls, burning with passion. Now, truly himself and confident, he agreed to be guided by a pulsating fantasy that was simultaneously Shakespearean and Neo-Platonic.

This state of mind alone drove Picasso during this period. An example will shed some light on his working methods.

After a beautiful series of metaphysical acrobats, ballerinas serving Diana, enchanting clowns, and "Harlequins Trismegistus,"[83] Picasso had painted, without a model, the very pure and very simple image of a young Parisian workman. Beardless and dressed in blue cloth, he almost resembled the artist himself when he was at work.

One night, Picasso deserted the company of his friends who were wasting their time with intellectual palaver. He returned to his studio and taking up the canvas that had been abandoned for a month, crowned the effigy of the little artisan with roses. Through a sublime caprice, he had transformed his work into a masterpiece.[84]

Picasso could have continued to live and work in this manner, happy and rightfully self-satisfied. There was no need to exert himself further in the hopes of receiving more praise or a faster increase in his fortune, because his canvases were beginning to be sought after.

Nevertheless, Picasso was restless. He turned his canvases to the wall and threw down his brushes.

---

[83] Salmon refers to the last verse in Apollinaire's "Crépuscule" in *Alcools*: "Le nain regarde d'un air triste/Grandir l'arlequin trismégiste" (The dwarf looks on in a sad pose/How Harlequin Trismégiste grows). "Harlequin Trismegistus" is a synthesis of the two characters Harlequin, the artful ladies' man of commedia dell'arte and Hermes Trismegistus, the "thrice great Hermes," a Greek god associated with the Egyptian god Thoth—patron of wisdom and learning. Hermes Trismegistus invokes thoughts about mysticism and alchemy. Harlequin was Picasso's alter ego in his art since 1901. Here Salmon brings out the mystical feeling surrounding Picasso's Harlequins from the Rose Period, often seen with their families or fellow performers, sometimes at home, sometimes in a vacant, eerie landscape (e.g., *Family of Saltimbanques*, 1905, National Gallery, Washington, DC). [BGN]

[84] The painting is *Boy with a Pipe*, autumn 1905, formerly in Collection of Mrs. John Hay Whitney, currently in a private collection. Further consideration of *Boy with a Pipe* is offered in my "André Salmon, Pablo Picasso and the History of Cubism," *André Salmon, poète de l'Art vivant, Var et Poésie* 8 (Toulon-Var: Université du Sud, 2010, pp 295-308). [BGN]

During long days, and so many nights, he drew, concretizing the abstract and reducing the concrete to its essentials.[85] Never was labor compensated with so little joy. Devoid of his recent youthful enthusiasm, Picasso undertook a large canvas which was to become the first application of his research.

The artist was already passionately fond of the Africans and placed them well above the Egyptians. His enthusiasm was not based on a vain appetite for the picturesque. Polynesian or Dahomeyan images seemed "rational" to him. Renewing his work, Picasso inevitably would give us an appearance of the world that did not conform to the way we learned how to see it.

The intimate visitors to the curious studio on the rue Ravignan, who had confidence in the young master, were generally disappointed when he permitted them to judge the first stage of his new work.[86]

This canvas has never been exhibited in public.[87] It includes six large female nudes[88] drawn with a marked crudeness. For the first time in Picasso's work, the expression of the faces is neither tragic nor passionate. They are about being masks, released, for the most part, from any humanity. However, these figures are not gods, neither Titans nor heroes; they are not even allegorical or symbolic. They are naked problems—white ciphers on a blackboard.

The sober principle of the painting-equation has just been laid down.

---

[85] The best source on Picasso's drawings from this period and their importance in the development of Cubism is Pepe Karmel, *Picasso and the Invention of Cubism* (New Haven: Yale University Press, 2003). [BGN]

[86] Salmon refers to *Les Demoiselles d'Avignon* (Museum of Modern Art, New York), begun in the spring of 1907. It was completed by the end of the year. [BNG]

[87] *Les Demoiselles d'Avignon* was not exhibited publicly until July 1916, when Salmon gave the painting its present title and included it in the Salon d'Antin. [BGN]

[88] Salmon is mistaken here. *Les Demoiselles d'Avignon* has five figures. It may be that Salmon had not seen the painting for quite some time when he wrote this book in 1912, since it was often covered with a cloth—we can see this in photographs of Picasso's studio (see note 18). Most likely, Salmon relied on his memory. In Picasso's early sketches for the painting, he had included two additional figures: a medical student entering the room on the left side and a sailor seated among the posing prostitutes. [BGN]

Picasso's new canvas was spontaneously baptized "The Philosophical B[rothel]" by a friend of the artist.[89] That was, I believe, the last studio joke the circle of these young innovative painters would cheerfully enjoy. Painting, henceforth, became a science and not one of the least austere.

Salon d'Automne, Salon XI, Grand Palais des Champs-Elyseese, Paris,

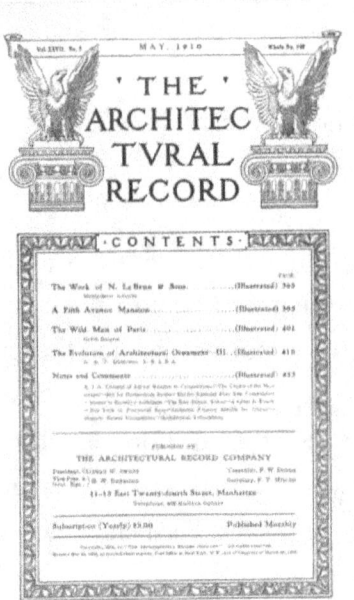

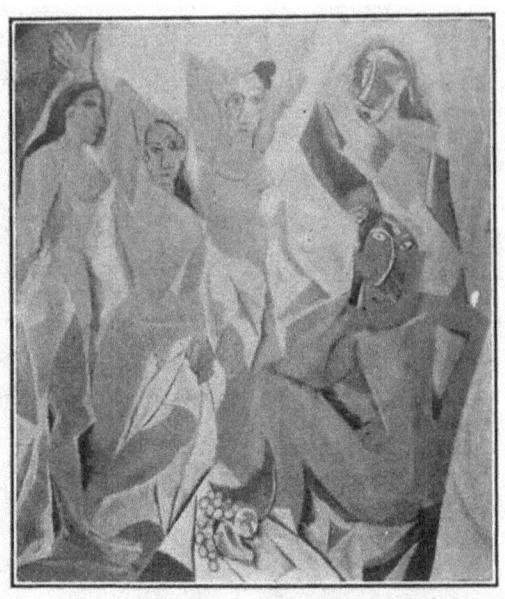

Study by Picasso.

Figure 9. Gelett Burgess, "The Wild Men of Paris," *Architectural Record*, May 1910

---

[89] In *Propos d'Atelier* (Paris: G. Crès, 1922), 16, Salmon wrote that he, Max Jacob (1876–1944) and Guillaume Apollinaire (1880–1918) called the painting, *Le B . . . philosophique*. William Rubin claims that Picasso called the painting his "bordel" (William Rubin, "The Genesis of *Les Demoiselle d'Avignon*," in *Les Demoiselles d'Avignon* [New York: The Museum of Modern Art, 1994], 122). See also the catalogue for the exhibition "*Les Demoiselles d'Avignon*" au Musée Picasso (Paris: Réunion des musées nationaux, 1988). [BGN]

II

The large canvas of severe, unlighted figures did not remain in its first state for a long time.

Soon Picasso attacked the faces whose noses were, for the most part, situated frontally in the form of isosceles triangles. The sorcerer's apprentice continued to consult the Oceanian and African enchanters.

Shortly afterward, these noses appeared white and yellow. A few touches of blue and yellow created relief on some of the bodies. Picasso composed a limited palette of sharp tones that corresponded exactly to schematic drawing.

Finally, unhappy with his first research, he attacked other nudes—spared until then, having been set aside by this Neronian[90] who was searching for a new laws and composing his palette with pinks, whites and various tones of gray.

For a short time, Picasso appeared to be pleased with that development. The "philosophical b[rothel]" was turned to the wall. At the same time, he painted those canvases with beautiful tonal harmony and such a supple drawing—most often nudes, which made up the content of Picasso's last exhibition in 1910.[91]

This painter, who had been the first to know how to restore some nobility to the discredited subject, returned to the "study" and studies of his first style: *Woman at Her Toilette*, and *Woman Combing Her Hair*—thus seeming, for an

---

[90] This is an allusion to the great conflagration in Rome of 64 CE, when it was suspected that Emperor Nero had ordered the setting of these fires in certain neighborhoods so that he would have the power to reconstruct them. [JG]

[91] Guillaume Apollinaire wrote in *L'Intransigeant* on December 21, 1910, that the Vollard Gallery exhibition consisted of paintings done "some time ago." On December 23 he noted that some "characteristic" works were added. In *Les Marches de Provence*, February 1911, he described Picasso's works in this show as "fathomless" blues and "recent rose paintings." (Leroy C. Breunig, ed., *Apollinaire on Art: Essays and Reviews*, translated by Susan Suleiman [New York: Da Capo, 1972], 122–123, 196). [BGN]

instant, to give up any further gains from the research that made him sacrifice his original gifts of immediate seduction.[92]

We must follow step by step the man who would be taken away by a tragic curiosity until he brought about Cubism. A vacation interrupted his painful experiments.[93] Upon his return, Picasso again picked up the large experimental canvas, which, as I have said, lived only through its figures.

In it he created atmosphere through a dynamic decomposition of luminous power; an effort that left the endeavors of Neo-Impressionism and Divisionism far behind. Geometric signs—a geometry at once infinitesimal and cinematic—appeared as the principal element for a style of painting whose development nothing could stop from then on.

It was Picasso's fate he never would, nor ever could, become again a prolific, innocent and learned creator of human poetry.

---

[92] *Woman at Her Toilette/ La Toilette*, spring–summer 1906 (Albright-Knox Gallery, Buffalo) and *Woman Combing Her Hair*, summer-autumn 1906 (Museum of Modern Art, New York, entitled *Woman Plaiting her Hair*). [BGN]

[93] There is no known evidence that Picasso (1881–1973) left Paris during the summer of 1907. A letter dated August 8 from Fernande Olivier (1881–1966) to Gertrude Stein (1874–1946), then in Fiesole, Italy, indicates that Picasso, Fernande and Salmon were at that time in Paris. (Hélène Seckel and Judith Cousins, "Chronology," in *Demoiselles d'Avignon* [New York: Museum of Modern Art, 1994], 152) Salmon seems to have confused Picasso's 1906 vacation in Gosol with 1907. [BGN] John Richardson said, however (*A Life of Picasso*, II, 1996, 40), "Although Picasso explicitly denied taking the slightest time off at this time, it is possible that he paid a visit to the country in the course of this summer." This could have been a short stay in the Haute-Garonne at Eugène Rouart's home at the end of July–beginning of August—not a long vacation such as the one he took the previous summer in Spain. [JG]

III

Those inclined to consider the Cubists audacious jokers or shrewd dealers might deign to take note of all the drama that truly presides over the birth of this art.

Picasso himself had also "meditated on geometry,"[94] and while he chose savage artists as leaders, he did not ignore their barbarity. Only he conceived logically that they had attempted the real figuration of existence and not the realization of the idea, most often sentimental, that we make of it.

Those who see in Picasso's work signs of the occult, the symbolic or the mystical greatly risk never understanding him.

Thus, he wants to give us a total representation of man and things. That is what the barbarian artists attempt to do. But here it is about painting itself,[95] about art on a surface, and that is why Picasso, in his turn, has to create these balanced figures outside the laws of academicism and an anatomical system, while situating them in a space rigorously conforming to the unforeseen freedom of their movements.

The decision to create in such a way is enough to make the person who pursues it the foremost artist of his age—even if he were to experience only the bitter joy of research without harvesting its fruit.

The results of the original research were disconcerting. There was no concern for grace; taste was repudiated as too narrow a measure!

Nudes were born whose deformation was hardly surprising since we were prepared by Picasso himself, Matisse, Derain, Braque, van Dongen, and, before that, Cézanne and Gauguin. It was the hideousness of the faces that froze with horror the half-converted.

Deprived of the smile, we could only recognize the grimace.

---

[94] Salmon refers to Charles Baudelaire, who depicted himself as "méditant sur la géométrie" in "Les Petites Vieilles" ("Little Old Women"), pièce XCI in *Les Fleurs du Mal*, 1861. [JG]

[95] The African image-makers were sculptors. Here Salmon emphasizes Picasso's approach as a painter. [JG]

Perhaps, the smile of the *Mona Lisa* was the Sun of Art for too long.

Her adoration corresponds to some particularly depressing, supremely demoralizing, decadent Christianity. One could say, paraphrasing Arthur Rimbaud, that the *Mona Lisa*, the eternal *Mona Lisa*, was a thief of energies.[96]

It is difficult not to reflect in favor of the innovator if we put face to face one of the nudes and one of the still lifes from this instant of Picassism (Cubism not having been invented yet).

Whereas the human effigy appears to us so inhuman and inspires some sort of fear, we can more easily subject our sensibility to the evident and quite new beauties of the representation of that loaf of bread or that violin or that cup—never before painted in such a way.

It is because the accepted appearance of these objects is less dear to us than our own representation, our reflection distorted in the mirror of intelligence.

Thus, with desperate confidence, we will agree to be dragged into the search under the guidance of Picasso or some other painter in his family.

Will much time be wasted? This is the problem!

Who will demonstrate the necessity, the superior esthetic reason for painting beings and things such as they are and not as our eye has recognized

---

[96] Here Salmon rephrases Arthur Rimbaud's (1854–1891) "Les Premières Communions" ("First Communions", 1871), part 9: "Christ! ô Christ, éternel voleur des énergies" ("Christ! Oh, Christ, eternal thief of energies"). [BGN]

The *Mona Lisa* was quite fashionable at that time. On Sunday, August 21, 1911, it was stolen from the Louvre. While Salmon wrote *La Jeune Peinture française* the painting had not been recovered. Salmon's close friend Guillaume Apollinaire had employed as a secretary a shady character named Géry Pieret, who boasted that he stole in 1907 two Iberian heads that had belonged to the Louvre. Picasso bought those very heads. Fearing their discovery at the time of the *Mona Lisa* theft, Picasso arranged to return the sculptures anonymously through Salmon's newspaper *Paris-Journal*. Because of his connection to Pieret, Apollinaire was arrested on September 8 and released from jail on September 12. At that time, Picasso denied knowing Apollinaire when questioned by the police. His name was not on *Paris-Journal*'s petition to exonerate Apollinaire (Judith Cousins of the Museum of Modern Art, New York, pointed this out to me for my previous study of Salmon). The *Mona Lisa* was recovered in Florence, in November 1913. [BGN]

them. That is to say, not since the beginning of time, but since men meditated on our image?

Is that not art itself?

Is not science the single guide for these researchers, who worry about subjecting us to all the angles of a prism at once, and blend touch and sight, the two sources of many disparate joys?

To that question, no one has yet been able to respond in a decisive way.

On the other hand, the concern to make us feel an object's total existence is not absurd in itself. The world changes its appearance. We no longer have the mask of our fathers, and our sons will not resemble us. Nietzsche wrote: "We have made the earth very small, say the last men, and they blink."[97] Terrible prophecy! Is not the salvation of the soul on earth depending on a completely new art?

To that, I do not intend to respond today, as I am only aiming to prove that some artists, unjustly abused, obeyed ineluctable laws whose anonymous genius bears the responsibility.

This chapter is nothing other than an anecdotal history of Cubism.

Nothing that I advance here is ill-considered. As early as 1910, Mr. Jean Metzinger confided to a reporter: "We had never had the curiosity to touch the objects we were painting."[98]

---

[97] From Friedrich Nietzsche's (1844–1900) *Thus Spoke Zarathustra*: "The earth has become small, and on it hops the last man who makes everything small. His race is as ineradicable as the flea-beetle; the last man lives longest. 'We have invented happiness,' say the last men, and they blink." (Friedrich Nietzsche, *Thus Spoke Zarathustra*, in *The Portable Nietzsche*, translated by Walter Kaufman [New York: Viking Press, 1954, repr. 1968], 129.) [BGN]

[98] Jean Metzinger, "Note sur la peinture," *Pan*! (October–November 1910), 649–51. [BGN]

IV

But Picasso returned to his military-drill-ground of a canvas. He had to test the accent of a new palette. The artist found himself in a truly tragic position. He still had no disciples (and of those future disciples, several would become hostile ones), while some painter friends distanced themselves from him. Conscious of their weakness and fearful of the example, they hated the clever snares of intelligence (others without my scruples could cite their names). The studio on the rue Ravignan was no longer the "meeting place of poets."[99] The new ideal separated the men who were beginning to look at each other "from all sides at once," and learned thus to scorn each other.

Somewhat abandoned, Picasso took the advice again from the African soothsayers. He composed for himself a palette rich in all the tones dear to the old academics: ocher, bitumen and sepia, and painted several formidable nudes, grimacing and perfectly worthy of execration.[100]

But with what singular nobility Picasso clothes all that he touches!

The monsters of his mind drive us to despair, but they will never shake the most vulgar among us with that democratic laughter which brings about the Sunday crowd's invasion at the Indépendants'.

Already the Prince-Alchemist, this Picasso who makes us think of Goethe, Rimbaud and Claudel, was no longer alone.

---

[99] Picasso had written in blue chalk on his Bateau-Lavoir studio's door "Au rendez-vous des Poètes" in honor of Max Jacob, Salmon and Apollinaire who would meet at this place almost every evening. Here Salmon alludes to a quarrel between Jacob and Apollinaire, referred to in a note from Max to Picasso, dated June 6, 1909: "I am on very bad terms with Apollinaire who acted like a boor." See *Max Jacob et Picasso*, Réunion des musées nationaux, 1994, 70. [JG]

[100] *Three Women*, 1907–early 1909, The State Hermitage Museum, St. Petersburg. [BGN] Picasso photographed Salmon standing in front of this painting in his Bateau-Lavoir studio. See Hélène Seckel [Klein], "Portrait de poètes," in *Picasso and the Portrait*, Flammarion and Réunion des musées nationaux, 1996, 182; New York: Museum of Modern Art, 1996, 182. [JG]

Jean Metzinger, Robert Delaunay and Georges Braque became peculiarly interested in his work.

Let us admit right away that André Derain would join him through personal paths, to go his own way shortly after, without surpassing him. At least, Picasso instilled in him the need to desert the conversational salon connected to Henri Matisse's studio.

Vlaminck, a giant with loyal and categorical thoughts like the straight punch of a good boxer, was losing (not without amazement) his conviction to be a typical Fauve. He had never imagined that one could exceed in audacity the violence of the sorrowful Vincent van Gogh. He returned to Chatou, mulling it over, but not convinced.

Jean Metzinger and Robert Delaunay painted landscapes planted with little houses reduced to the severe appearance of parallelepipeds. Living a less inward life than Picasso, remaining painters more on the surface than their predecessor, these young artists were in much more of a hurry to accomplish their goals—albeit in a less complete fashion.

Their great haste determined the success of the enterprise.

Once exhibited, their works passed almost unnoticed by the public and the art critics, who—green cap or blue cap, Guelph and Ghibelline, Montague and Capulet—recognized only the Fauves, whether to praise or curse them.[101]

---

[101] Pro-Catholics wore blue caps (the color of the Virgin) and anti-Catholics wore green caps. This opposition reappears more clearly at the end of "L'Église dans le brouillard," in Salmon's collection of prose and poems, *Le Manuscrit trouvé dans un chapeau*, a book accompanied by numerous Picasso drawings (Paris: Société littéraire de France, 1919; repr. Fata Morgana, 1983), 25. [JG] In Italy and Germany, the Guelphs and Ghibellines were aristocratic families and political parties who opposed each other from the middle ages into the late Renaissance. The Guelphs (originally the Germanic Welf) supported the Pope and based their wealth on mercantile interests. The Ghibellines supported the Holy Roman Empire and based their wealth on agriculture. The Montagues and Capulets are the feuding families in Shakespeare's *Romeo and Juliet*. [BGN]

Yet, Henri Matisse, king of the Fauves, who had just been crowned in Berlin,[102] threw out of the family, with one word, Jean Metzinger and Robert Delaunay. Was it rashness or political skill?

With this feminine sense of the appropriate, from which his taste is formed, he baptized these two artists' little houses "Cubist." An ingenious or ingenuous art critic, who was accompanying him, ran to his newspaper, dashed off the gospel article and the next day the public learned of the birth of Cubism.[103]

Schools disappear for want of convenient labels. It is distressing for the public, because it likes schools which allow it to see clearly without effort. The public quite docilely accepted Cubism, even going so far as to recognize Picasso as the leader of the school and standing firm in that belief.

Since then, the misunderstanding has only increased.

Georges Braque, who a few months earlier painted brutal landscapes in Vlaminck's style and was also interested in Seurat's discoveries, did not contribute insignificantly to confirming the double mistake.

---

[102] In 1908, Matisse visited Munich, Heidelberg and Berlin with his student Hans Purrmann (1880–1966). He exhibited at Paul Cassirer's gallery in Berlin that year. Matisse exhibited with the Berlin Secession and in Düsseldorf at the Sunderbund exhibition in spring and fall 1910, respectively, and returned to Munich with Purrmann and Albert Marquet in October 1910 (John Elderfield, *Henri Matisse: A Retrospective* [New York: Museum of Modern Art, 1992], 183). [BGN]

[103] Salmon's explanation for the origin of the word "Cubism" bridges two separate incidents: The word "cube" used in connection with Robert Delaunay's (1885–1941) and Jean Metzinger's (1883–1956) work appears in Louis Chassevent's review "22ᵉ Salon des Indépendants, 1906," *Quelques petits salons* (Paris, 1908), 32; in Daniel Robbins, "Jean Metzinger: At the Center of Cubism," *Jean Metzinger in Retrospect* (Iowa City: University of Iowa Museum of Art, 1985), 11. The word "cubes" appears in Louis Vauxcelles' review of Georges Braque's (1882–1963) exhibition at Kahnweiler's gallery in November 1908 (Louis Vauxcelles, "Exposition Braque. Chez Kahnweiler, 28 rue Vignon," *Gil Blas*, November 14, 1908). The word "Cubism" appeared for the first time in print in Charles Morice's review of the Salon des Indépendants, *Mercure de France*, April 16, 1909 (Beth S. Gersh-Nesic, *The Early Criticism of André Salmon: A Study of his Thoughts on Cubism* [New York: Garland Publishing, 1991], 97). [BGN]

He joined Jean Metzinger and Robert Delaunay. But, preoccupied with the human figure earlier than the latter two, he borrowed directly from Picasso— although at the time there was room in his work for a modest expression of his own sensibility.

Later, he was to follow him, respectfully, step by step, allowing one often judicious critic to write those excessive words: "They say that the inspiration for the movement is from Mr. Picasso, but since he does not exhibit at all, we must consider Mr. Georges Braque as the true representative of the new school."[104]

Much more intellectual, Mr. Jean Metzinger, painter and poet (an author of beautiful esoteric verse), wanted to justify this Cubism (created by Henri Matisse, who did not participate in the enterprise) and thought of gathering the confused elements of the doctrine.[105]

So, if in fact Cubism (baptized by Henri Matisse) comes from Picasso (who did not practice it), Jean Metzinger is entitled to be called its leader. However, he quickly conceded: "Cubism is a means, not an end." Ergo: Cubism is wonderful because it does not exist, although it has been invented by four people.

Today, we see the Cubists separate from each other more and more. Little by little, they are giving up the small gimmicks they employed cooperatively. What they called discipline was only, in essence, a form of gymnastics, something like *la culture plastique*.[106]

---

[104] Michel Puy, "Les Indépendants," *Les Marges* (July 1911), 27–30. [BGN]

[105] Jean Metzinger, "Cubisme et Tradition," *Paris-Journal* (August 18, 1911), 5. [BGN]

[106] A play on the commonly known expression "la culture physique" and its craze. The cult of the body beautiful and eugenics had its zenith in France and in Germany during the early decades of the twentieth century (Fay Brauer, "Building the Body Beautiful: `La Culture Physique' and the New Artistic Anatomy in the French Radical Republic," CAA Conference, New York, February 26, 2000). [BGN]

We thought we were in the Academy, but we are leaving the Gym.[107]

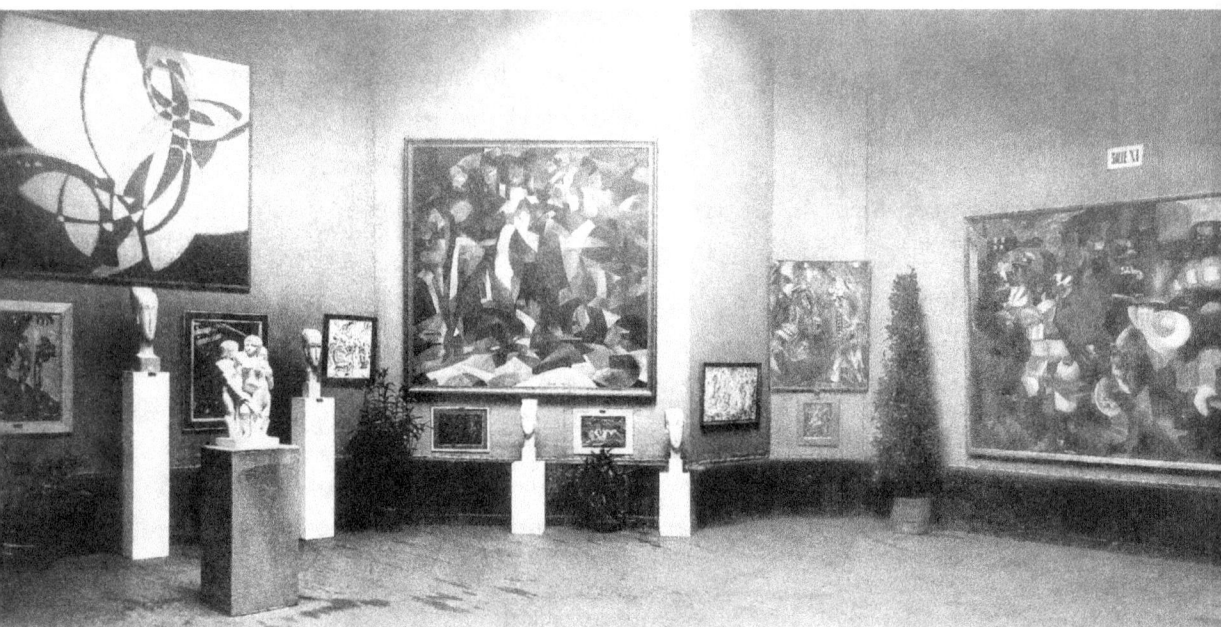

Figure 10. Salon d'Automne, Salon XI, Grand Palais des Champs-Elysées, Paris, October 1 and November 8, 1912, Photograph: Public Domain.

---

[107] [107]The French word *Gymnase* doesn't mean Gymnasium, a secondary school with a classical curriculum; it is the place for physical training. [JG] Salmon may refer here to Henri Le Fauconnier's appointment to chef d'école of the Académie de la Palette, led by Jacques-Émile Blanche (1861–1942) since 1902. Jean Metzinger and André Dunoyer de Segonzac became instructors. In his column "Courrier des Ateliers," *Paris-Journal*, February 8, 1912, page 4, under the rubric "Academism," Salmon announced the transition at this well-known progressive art school in the 5th arrondissement. Noted alumni are Marc Chagall, Nadezhda Udaltsova and Sonia Turk-Delaunay, among many others. [BGN]

V

While Jean Metzinger and Robert Delaunay (somewhat linked for a while), and Georges Braque (on the other hand, isolated) were providing art criticism with works that were considered the school's achievements, Picasso and André Derain (who were not exhibiting) worked independently: the former directly pursuing his studies, the latter distancing himself more and more from the dogma.

Picasso composed a new palette of grays, blacks, whites and greens, which, adopted right away by Georges Braque, became that of all the Cubists.[108]

At this time the school grew larger: first through Le Fauconnier,[109] who was an individualist, transforming all that he had received, an authoritarian, too, in his affections and, in that way, very much like Matisse whom he rejected; then through Albert Gleizes, who joined the chorus of theorizers with no intention of renouncing forever terrestrial plenitude altogether.[110]

---

[108] Picasso seems to have reduced his palette to browns and greens during the fall–winter of 1907 in his first studies of *Three Women*. Braque reduced his palette to browns and sepias during the winter of 1908. For a full account of the relationship between Picasso and Braque during the development of Cubism see William Rubin et al., *Picasso and Braque: Pioneering Cubism* (New York: Museum of Modern Art, 1989). [BGN]

[109] Henri Le Fauconnier (1881–1946) published his personal vision for Cubism in the catalogue *Das Kunstwerk,* for an exhibition of the same name organized in Munich by the Neue Kunstlervereinigung (NKV). It was their second exhibition, which opened in September 1910. Le Fauconnier's ideas predate Metzinger's similar ideas, published in *Pan!* (October–November 1910). Le Fauconnier presided over the "Salon Cubists" who emerged at the Salon des Indépendants in 1911: Jean Metzinger, Albert Gleizes, Ferdinand Léger, etc. [BGN]

[110] Albert Gleizes (1881–1953) and Jean Metzinger published their ideas in *Du Cubisme* (Paris: Eugène Figuière, 1912). The book was made available to the public on December 27, 1912. Salmon's *La Jeune Peinture française*, completed in April, was available in October 1912. [BGN]

Fernand Léger, still settled into a quiet academy, was waking up to a prouder form of art with great astonishment.[111]

Everything I have just summarized of the brief but abundant history of Cubism is totally unknown by the public and a great number of the most informed art lovers.

I have not guessed at anything. Fate simply assigned to me the role of witness, and I am now trying my hand at a faithful testimony.

The ignorance of the favorable circumstances which gave birth to Cubism explains rather well enough the muddle of ideas that persisted until the Salon d'Automne of 1911.

Encouraged by the assistant district attorney Mr. Granié (deputy general counsel for the new school), Mr. Desvallières[112] (a convert to Cubism without practicing it, much like Mr. Charles Maurras[113] defends the Roman Catholic Church) was the first to have the idea of assembling in one room dissimilar works—linked, however, as they showed the same frame of mind that was shared by Messrs. Jean Metzinger, Le Fauconnier, Albert Gleizes, Fernand Léger, N. de la Fresnaye, Duchamp, Dunoyer de Segonzac, André Lhote,

---

[111] Fernand Léger was born in 1881 (as were Picasso and Salmon) in Normandy where his father raised cattle. He studied at the free academies in Paris, in particular the quiet Académie Julian. His first significant work was *Nudes in a Forest* (Rijksmuseum Kröller-Müller, Otterlo), which was exhibited in the Salon des Indépendants in 1911. He died in 1955. [JG]

[112] Georges Desvallières (1861–1950) was a student of Gustave Moreau (1826–1898) and close friend of Maurice Denis (1870–1943). His influence on the jury for the Salon d'Automne of 1911 brought this controversial group of Cubists into the exhibition and secured a separate room for their work. In 1919, he founded the Studio for Sacred Arts. He is known for his frescos and stained-glass windows. The "substitut Granié" was a deputy attorney general who supported the avant-garde in critiques that he wrote under the name Aloysius Duravel (Richardson, *Life of Picasso*, II, 207). Linked to Albert Gleizes, he helped Apollinaire in the Mona Lisa affair. [JG]

[113] Polemicist, founder of the extreme-rightist journal *L'Action française*, Charles Maurras (1868–1952) advocated for the return of the monarchy and accused the Republic of being taken over by Protestants, Jews and Freemasons. He supported the Roman Catholic Church for strictly political reasons and was condemned by the pope in 1926. [JG]

Albert Moreau, Fontenay,[114] etc. These artists would soon be followed by Herbin and the sensitive Juan Gris.[115]

This mosaic of works was criticized. The lack of unity is explained by the default of Georges Braque and Robert Delaunay, from whom some characteristic entries were awaited and who instead gave up their corner of the wall to members of another movement, while André Marchand was forgotten in the vicinity of Maurice Denis.

No matter. This error was a trifle. The great blow had been struck. It was no longer possible to ignore Cubism.

It was either admired or derided. Air was in short supply in Room VIII. Writers talked about a rebirth, about the salvation of art. Others beseeched their colleagues not to favor a national peril. Very few were set on despising the work or satisfied with facetious remarks.

I limited my task to recognizing those artists in the Cubist family who were truly gifted with pictorial virtues.

But those who laughed, the strangers to art, would assure the success of this exhibition.

Thus Neo-Impressionism, popularly known as Pointillism, became famous ten years after its revelation, when Willette, a charming artist and singular rebel against anything to do with the mind (he is all sentiment), drew a Pierrot as a painter crying out: "Curses! I'm painting with confetti!"[116]

---

[114] Contrary to the other painters mentioned here by Salmon, Charles de Fontenay (1889–1916) is not well known. He is one of the young painters who died on the battlefield in World War I. [JG]

[115] Cubism was launched officially in the famous Room 41 in the Salon des Indépendants of April–May 1911. Here Salmon talks about the juried Salon d'Automne, late September-October 1911, where the Salon Cubists were grouped together in Room VIII. [BGN]

[116] Adolphe Willette (1867–1926), painter, designer and humorist, was one of the iconic personalities among the Montmartre bohemians. He decorated numerous cabarets frequented by the painters (Toulouse-Lautrec, Pissarro, Seurat, Signac, etc.), such as Le Moulin Rouge or Le Chat Noir. He used the character Pierrot, which appeared in a great deal of his caricatures as a sort of alter ego. He founded the journal *Le Pierrot* (1889–1891) and published his memoirs under the title *Feu Pierrot* [*The Late Pierrot*] in 1919. [JG]

The anger of certain people left the fury of the anti-Wagnerians far behind. As in the distressing days of the Dreyfus Affair,[117] discord divided families and old friendships were destroyed.

Now, just as Cubism was beginning to gain attention so keenly that it posed a new social question for many people, the school—brand new—was beginning to break up, each one going his own way.

The last to come along, Fernand Léger, seemed to have rallied the main body of the troop only to proclaim a schism. So, he was credited with Tubism. Fernand Léger was to waste little time before returning to more profound studies.

All renounced unity of coloration; all smashed Picasso's palette.

Albert Gleizes was no longer bothered by anecdote and Jean Metzinger, with a great expenditure of his talent, rehabilitated grace among his own followers. In response to the grimacing idols, worshiped of late, he countered with a sort of *Mona Lisa* of Cubism.[118]

---

[117] In 1894, Captain Alfred Dreyfus (1859–1935), a French Jew from Alsace, was the victim of a judicial error perpetrated by a military tribunal, which found him guilty of treason and sent him to a penal colony. This incident launched an enormous political crisis, dividing public opinion into two camps: those who supported the verdict and those who felt Dreyfus was innocent. The great Naturalist novelist Émile Zola (1840–1902) supported Dreyfus in the name of human rights, which forced him into self-exile in London in order to avoid imprisonment. Tried and condemned again by court martial in 1899, Dreyfus was eventually pardoned by the French President Émile Loubet (1838–1929). In 1906 he was exonerated and reinstated in the French Army where he served as a major through World War I. [JG]

[118] Jean Metzinger's *Le Goûter* [*Femme à la cuiller*] *(Teatime* [*Woman with a Teaspoon*]), 1911 (Philadelphia Museum of Art). The picture was exhibited in the 1911 Salon d'automne, right after theft of the *Mona Lisa* from the Louvre. In his "Courrier des ateliers" *Paris-Journal*, October 3, 1911, 5, Salmon [under the pseudonym *La Palette*] dubbed Metzinger's female figure in *Le Goûter* "the *Mona Lisa* of Cubism." [JG]

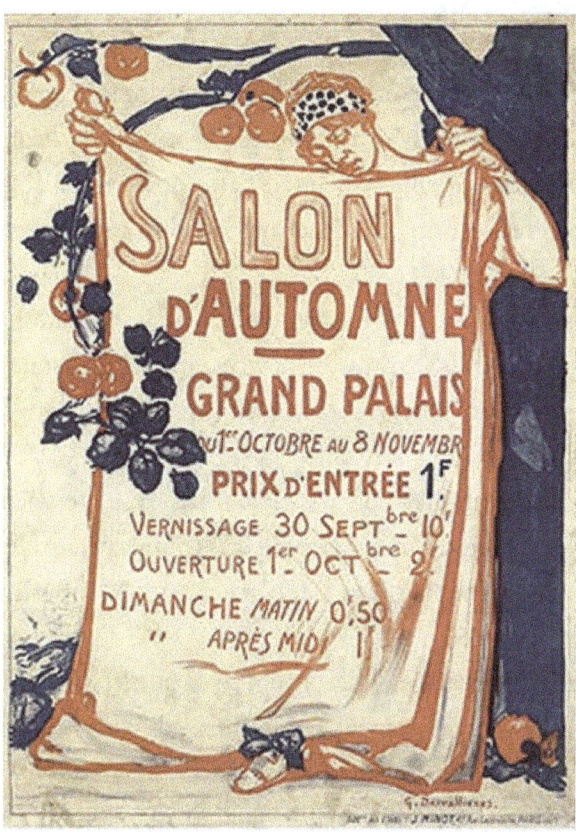

Figure 11. Salon d'Automne 1911

The New-York Times.

October 8, 1911

Eccentric School of Painting Increases Its Vogue in the Current Art Exhibition--- What Its Followers Attempt to Do.

AMONG all the paintings on exhibition at the Paris Fall Salon none is attracting so much attention as the extraordinary productions of the so-called "Cubist" school. In fact, dispatches from Paris suggest that these works are easily the main feature of the exhibition.

The "Cubists," be it known, are a school of artists who believe that the right way to paint persons and things is to paint them in cubes, squares, and lozenges. They have been before the public now for several years.

When they first burst on the astonished gaze of Paris and the rest of the universe they were known as the "Invertebrates." That was in 1905. On recovering from its first fit of amazement at the astonishing productions of the, "Invertebrates" the public promptly dubbed them the "Wild Beasts." Now they are "les Cubistes."

Whatever their name, they continue to paint pictures before which descriptive adjectives retreat in disorder. They slap colors, apparently in haphazard fashion, on their canvases, draw back a step, slap on another assortment, and then calmly label the sensational result "A Woman," "A Landscape," "Still Life," or something equally innocent and inadequate. If you seek to find out where they got their ideas you will learn that the "Invertebrates" and "Wild Beasts" and "Cubists" call themselves disciples of Matisse. But there are those who say that Matisse stands aghast before these madnesses.

In spite of the crazy nature of the "Cubist" theories the number of those professing them is fairly respectable. Georges Braque, André Derain, Picasso, Czobel, Othon Friesz, Herbin, Metzinger—these are a few of the names signed to canvases before which Paris has stood and now again stands in blank amazement.

What do they mean? Have those responsible for them taken leave of their senses? Is this art or madness? Who knows?

At all events the devoted group, advancing—or receding—year by year, can at least say that plenty of people waste time and adjectives upon them. If, like Kipling's "Bandar-Log," the foolish monkey-folk of the jungle, their desire is to be "noticed," they have been richly rewarded during their brief existence

Last year Gelett Burgess, he of "Purple Cow" fame, also known as an artist of eccentric habit, went to Paris and became inspired with a desire to find out something about this weird school. Perhaps the same twist of mind that caused him to turn out his sinuous and popular "Goops" moved him to undertake this voyage of discovery among hidden Parisian studios. Anyhow, he ventured forth on his quest, found what he sought, and described what he found in The Architectural Record.

The lust for discovery first stirred in Gelett Burgess when he entered the Salon des Indépendants and caught his first glimpse of a painting by one of the "Wild Men of Paris"—thus it is that he dubs those we know as "Cubists."

Here is how he describes that first glimpse:

"I had scarcely entered the Salon des Indépendants when I heard shrieks of

VI

Since then, each artist has steadfastly confirmed his position. Accepted Cubism has not triumphed, since the individual effort tends toward multiple evolutions. It will go on, but without ceasing to be modified. More susceptible to development than Neo-Impressionism, it will rather quickly cease to be what we believe it is now.

Painters far removed from the Cubists—their enemies even—will adopt a few of Le Fauconnier and his friends' expressive devices, for Degas' statement is still true and suits everyone: "They shoot us, and then dig through our pockets."[119]

Henri Matisse is alone. This celebrated man, enriched by art, a crowned painter, collected a following only in the suburbs: from Paris (more specifically in the Russo-American alleys of Montparnasse) and from Munich, Berlin and Moscow.

As for the other intransigent Fauves, I see them as disunited as the Cubists. And yet the birth of tomorrow's great painting needs a tight-knit and striking unity.

After many battles and sincere, strict, and laborious retreats, all end up mixed in together, despite themselves and without being aware of it, as in the days of 1904.

Already many students of the Fauves, without abandoning their mentors, are allying with the Cubists for important events.

Would Cubism be then only a subschool, a province of the Fauve realm, a realm formed by people stirred up by opposing needs and refusing to recognize the authority of the foreign prince whom fate has imposed upon them?[120]

Cubism will have at least restored the worship of the method.

---

[119] The noted authority on Edgar Degas, Richard Kendall suggested the following in response to an email query on this quotation: "The Degas quote mentioned by Salmon was one variation of a saying often cited among his followers. It was already a cliché by this date [1912]" (Email October 28, 2003). [BGN]

[120] Salmon means Picasso. [BGN]

Our task is simplified from now on. Without accounting for the absentees, deserters and fainthearted, we need only to examine the works of young painters breaking with academicism in any manner whatsoever.

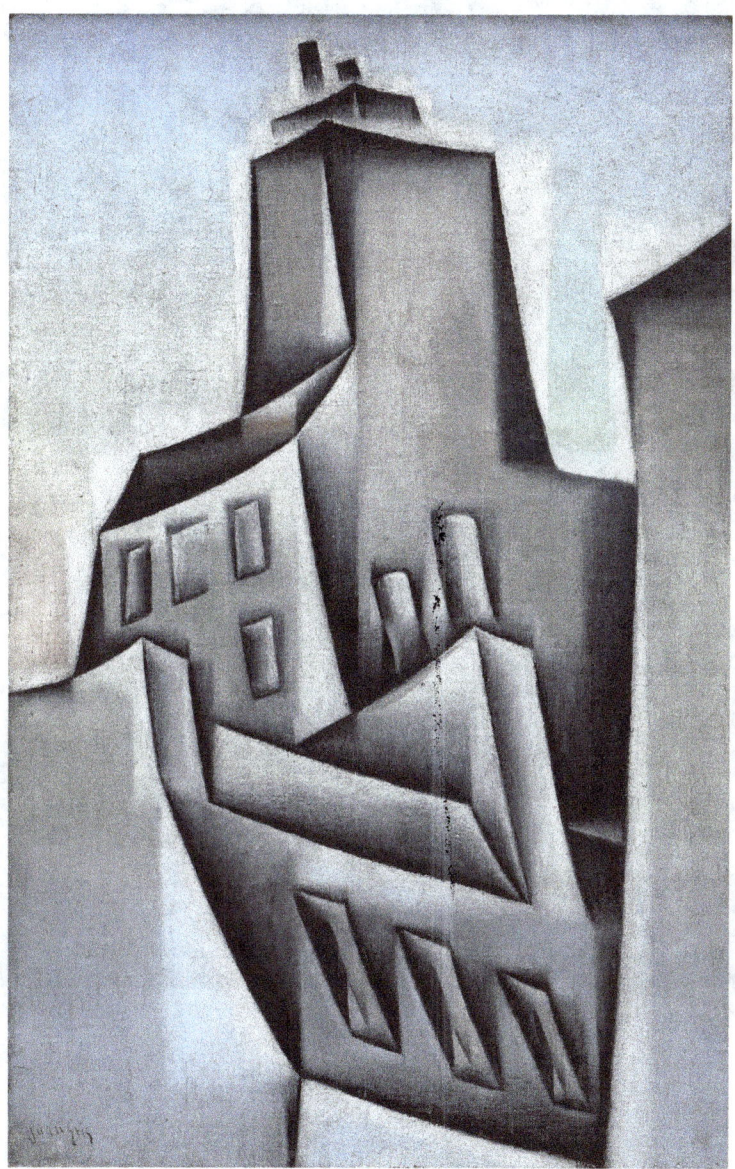

Figure 12. Juan Gris, *Houses in Paris*, 1911, Solomon R. Guggenheim Museum, New York.

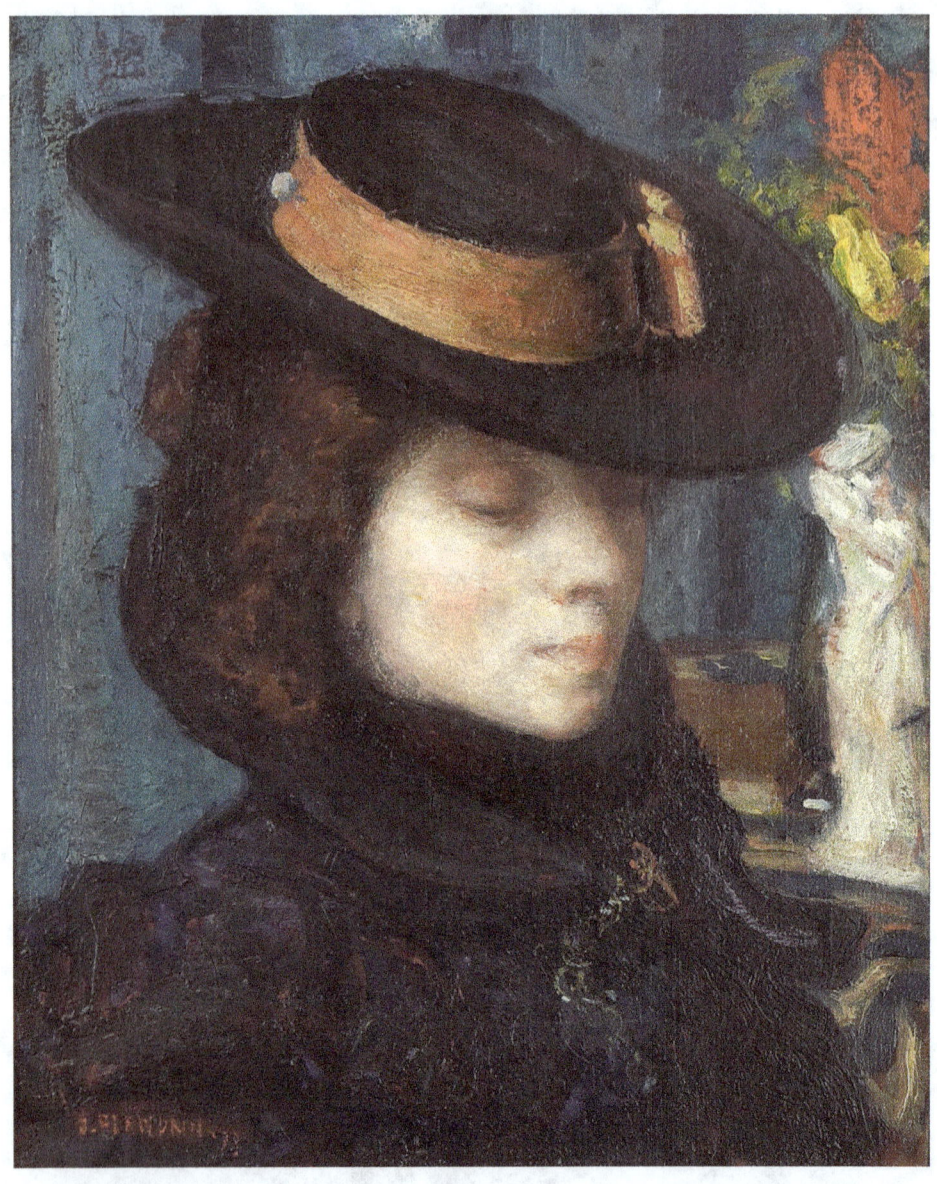

Figure 13. Jules Flandrin, *Portrait of Jacqueline Marval*, 1889

3

L'Art vivant[121]

In the future, the joy of studying a Jules Flandrin[122] may slip through our fingers. A recognized master by those in the know, his mastery will soon be revealed to the public.

The joy that imposes harmony and the wisdom that enlightens are the two great virtues of Jules Flandrin—a robust painter, and a lucid one too, such

---

[121] This concept is essential to Salmon who used it as the title for his book *L'Art vivant* (*Living Art*), published by Crès in 1920. He returns to the implication in the title *La Jeune Peinture française* (*Young French Painting*) of the image/art as an organism which develops and renews itself according to the laws of an internal growth, which conflict with the sociocultural weight of an ossified art that claims to keep up with and reside throughout the entire country. It plays a central role in the book *André Salmon poète de l'Art vivant* (*André Salmon, the Poet of Living Art*), a collection of essays edited by Michèle Monte in collaboration with Jacqueline Gojard, Université du Sud, Toulon-Var, *Var et Poésie*, no. 8, 2010. [JG]

[122] Gustave Moreau's student (along with Matisse and Marquet), Jules Flandrin (1871–1947) was the subject of a beautiful 1992 monograph by François Roussier (Éditions de l'association Flandrin Deloras). Works and themes recalled by Salmon appear in this book. [JG]

that he shares all his gifts without contradicting the necessary rules. Moreover, this generous discipline is native to the temperament of this mountaineer delighted with altitudes and sensitive to the peaceful charms of the valley.

The mountains, trees and herds are elements of poetry which he endears to us.

He paints tender and serious landscapes from which ascend the fragrances of the promised lands. Under a sky of deep blue stuffed with white clouds whose volume corresponds to the undulations of tranquil soil, he shows oxen descending from the Grand Chartreuse. He does not paint just "oxen," but a herd led by a serene and communal strength.

In other canvases, you see clouds of every gray tone tinted to violet rolling through a valley that feels already damp with the next rain.

Finally, Jules Flandrin knows how to compose a difficult painting of figures, the likes of which the *pompiers*[123] artists almost filled us with disgust. Look at one of his most famous canvases, *The Amazon:* dressed in gray, she mounts an elegant mare whose white breast is dappled with sunshine. Beauty and the Beast both express pride. The landscape seems to recede, while the Amazon and horse penetrate it, but in fact light descends before the figures.

Afterward, if we examine the *Three Young Dancing Shepherds*, in which one figure is playing a flute, we are smitten by the human frenzy of this composition accomplished without disorder or delirium.

The Italian landscapes, which Flandrin gladly interprets, do not perhaps have all the purity of those of Dauphiné.[124] In a foreign climate, he forces himself and his gifts dissipate a bit. However, his effort has not been without some exquisite successes, and we savor the southern light spattering delicate rocks, stirred up to the point of distress.

We know with what joyous lyricism Jules Flandrin has located certain theatrical scenes. The Russian dancers at the Chatelet have furnished him

---

[123] Late nineteenth-century academic artists (e.g., William-Adolphe Bouguereau, Jean-Léon Gérôme). [BGN]

[124] A southeast region of France, in the Alps, where the Chartreuse Mountains are located. [JG]

with the excuse to paint bright fairy tales wherein all is movement dispensing light.[125]

Beautiful still lifes, strong and sprightly, have to be added to Jules Flandrin's current work. They celebrate (not without gravity) that deep soul, lying low in the things which belong to our life.

I remember a *Pastoral Trophy* that mixed a flute, syrinx, and violin with garlands of oak between familiar furniture, which gently evokes the voluptuous silence of a poet's room.

〜

What charms us in Dufrenoy[126] is the surprise, which is always new. There are surprises in color (as in the *Court of the Vendramin Palace, Palace on the Grand Canal, Vase and Cloth* and *An Olive Tree in Siena*) and surprises in line (as in *Place des Vosges, Place de la Bastille, Perspective on the Morosini Palace* and *View of Siena*), among so many others. Surprises without endangering unity.

Dufrenoy has undertaken all the research that excites our modern artists to the point of anxiety. They are the most difficult to please, but for him it was delightful. He has lost nothing of his ingenuous gifts or his original freshness. Culture and taste—of which some heretics[127] went as far as to distrust—spared him from mortal traps. He also, to a large degree, puts thought into

---

[125] Beginning in 1909, the Ballets Russes, managed by the famous impresario Serge Diaghilev (1872–1929), was enormously successful in Paris and inspired numerous painters. See, in particular, Flandrin's *La Pavlova and Nijinski* (1910) in the François Roussier monograph, mentioned in note 122. [JG]

[126] Georges Dufrenoy (1870–1943) was a Post-Impressionist who—along with Bonnard, Vuillard, Marquet, Derain and Friesz—belonged to the group of artists handled by Galerie Druet. He was awarded the Carnegie Prize in Pittsburgh in 1929 and enjoyed a wonderful career in Europe and the United States. [JG]

[127] Probably an allusion to the sensational declarations of the Futurists who recommended, among other things, the demolition of museums and the expression, by any means possible, of "universal dynamism." The first exhibition in Paris of Italian Futurist Painters took place at Galerie Bernheim-Jeune, from February 5 to 25, 1912. [JG]

composition. However, he sacrificed nothing to it. He will triumph for having remained profoundly human.

His strength is penetrated with tenderness. His sensitivity is nourished with substantial observations, which create flavor and a particular life in each of his landscapes. Poet of Paris, he knows that the quality of air around a river (*Views from the Pont-Neuf*) is not the same as it is around the borders of the suburbs (*Place de la Bastille*). This *Place de la Bastille* is one of the most perfect pictures by Georges Dufrenoy. Scorning the *trompe l'oeil* style, he has filled the circular refuge of the plaza with lively people. So, he has painted a vertiginous gyroscope whose power animates all the rest. In the canvases of this painter, as in the masters', there is always an absolute point upon which depend both the balance and the grace of the composition.

Augustin Carrera[128] likes the light so much that he allows it at times to blind him. He is a Fauve who has remained faithful to Impressionism.

Too clever, he never paints with as much ardor as in this frequent state of blindness, and in order to paint, he leans on this detestable habit.

It is a great shame because this artist (whose glibness makes one think inevitably of most Gascon and Provençal poets[129]) is really gifted.

Too much lyricism without discipline harms the quality of the drawing and composition of this impetuous painter. Why does he have to give all his rapture and gestures an equal meaning?

If Carrera paints like Walt Whitman[130] versified (without moderation), it is no longer Southernism, but indeed the worst Americanism.

---

[128] Augustin Carrera (born in Madrid of French parents in 1878, he died in Paris in 1952). [JG]

[129] An allusion to Edmond Rostand's play *Cyrano de Bergerac*, which was tremendously successful in 1897. [JG]

[130] Walt Whitman (1819-1892), published *Leaves of Grass* numerous times, from 1855 to 1892, increasing from 12 untitled poems on 95 "leaves" to over 400 poems. Translated into French by Léon Bazalgette (1872-1928) in 1909, it seems to exemplify, for Salmon, the American indulgence in excess. [JG/BGN]

His nudes in sunlight are often only good Impressionist exercises. But when the spirit comes to the rescue of his hand, this painter is certainly capable of realizing works with a more rigorous drawing that is quite inclined to a more discrete blooming of colors.

⚬✿⚬

Naivety would be the first, the purest of an artist's gifts if the circumstances of modern life did not make naivety look precisely like something monstrous and enormously artificial. At best, there is only one Rousseau[131] each century.

For the most part, to be naive is to deliberately forbid oneself from submitting to the powers of order to such an extent that avoiding them is the equivalent of evading life itself.

Don't be deceived on that score. A certain culture, a pure taste for order, and a strictly moral, and not social, sense of virtue—which has its direct correspondence in art—brings along with it a quality quite akin to naivety, though it has still not been defined.

It is the freshness of conscience, the innocence of unadulterated knowledge. Deltombe's effort tends toward the conquest of this superior virtue, so much that meeting him in this final state, we seem to approach him for the first time.[132]

Mr. René Guilleré wrote about him: "His emotion is always simple: sometimes seriously sweet and thoughtfully tender—a tribute, if I may say, to the first inclination of his heart—most often derived from joy, a healthy, strong and obstinate joy."[133]

---

[131] Henri Rousseau, known as Le Douanier, "the customs officer."

[132] Salmon saw in Paul Deltombe (1878–1971), a friend of Matisse and Signac, an authentic painter and not a phony "naïf." [JG]

[133] René Guilleré (1877–1932) was an arts administrator and entrepreneur, the president of the Society of Artists/Decorators, and the founder of the Primavera Atelier. His wife, Charlotte Chauchet-Guilleré (1878–1964), was a furniture designer. [BGN]

Jean Dolent would have approved of Dusouchet's living in Belleville, a more propitious place for artists to work, with its still well-protected provincial neighborhoods, than Montmartre—which has been overtaken by hysterics, boxers and gypsies.[134]

When Dusouchet leaves his studio (where one sees Paris from the Grand Palais to the Institut de France), he goes to the country. Oh, not far—Plaine-Saint-Denis, Lilas or Romainville. Dusouchet is not curious about complicated landscapes, and he knows very well that the humblest plain, even if sullied, can offer pure lines. He does not ask anything more of nature.

A mystical poet, he is gifted with a very strong but ascetic imagination, if I dare say. He considers Traupmann's field[135] worthy of being Golgotha for

---

[134] Starting in 1910, Apollinaire and Salmon lamented the sketchy character of Montmartre, preferring instead Montparnasse. Pierre-Léon Dusouchet (1876–1936), a painter and a sculptor, worked in Belleville and remained in the neighborhood, hardly affected by Parisian urbanity. Jean Dolent (1835–1936) was a writer, art critic and collector, who lived in Belleville where he received his friends Paul Gauguin, Odilon Redon and Eugène Carrière. [JG]

[135] This expression refers to the location of the Traupmann crime which took place in Pantin, a northeast suburb of Paris, in July–August 1869. Jean-Baptiste Traupmann, an Alsatian, befriended Jean Kinck of Roubaix (French Flanders) and learned of his small fortune which he hoped to invest in his manufacturing business. Traupmann murdered Kinck before he arrived in Guebwiller, Kinck's native city, and then wrote to Kinck's wife in her husband's name asking her to send Kinck money. Traupmann then collected the money in Guebwiller posing as Jean Kinck. When Kinck's older son (by his first wife) Gustave arrived in Guebwiller for their prearranged rendezvous, everyone claimed that Jean had never arrived. Traupmann then lured Gustave Kinck and his stepmother Marie, plus the other five Kinck children, to the Hôtel du Nord in Paris with a note from Jean (the strange writing explained as the result of a sprained wrist). First Traupmann brought Gustave, and later the wife and children, to the same field in Pantin, promising to take them to see Jean. All the victims were brutally murdered. Traupmann nearly escaped to New York. He was arrested in Le Havre, waiting for the boat (Canadian Illustrated News, October 30, 1869, found at the Library and Archives Canada website: https://www.canadiana.ca/view/oocihm.8_06230_1/7?r=0&s=1 [BGN]

the raising of the cross with Jesus aloft, surrounded by sobbing holy women (he took as models some poor girls from an atrocious military zone).

We will be indebted to Dusouchet for trying to restore fresco, one of the purest types of painting.

A church decorated by Dusouchet would be bright and propitious for prayer.[136] An oasis of tranquility, one pictures it in the darkest neighborhood devoured by vice and misery, wherein reside tormented and sorrowful poor people like those whom the artist groups in his *Entombment, Lost Paradise,* or *Vision of Adam.*

When Rodin points out the urgent need to return to antique fresco in order to renounce the pasty canvas, one must admire how much an artist like Dusouchet was able to extract from the technique of the old masters.

Besides the perfection of his skill, we must like the thought that guides a sensitive worker's hand. And some verse from Verlaine and Louis Le Cardonnel[137] will sing in our memories. . .

The only artist whom we can contrast with Dusouchet today is more directly a disciple of Puvis de Chavannes. The feeling that animates him is evidently from a religious order, but not Christian. It is from a sacred art that leads to ecstasy, if not to prayer, by circuitous paths.

Putting this thought aside for a moment, the eulogies accorded to Dusouchet correspond exactly to Blanchet.[138]

---

[136] Along with Maurice Denis and Georges Desvallières, Dusouchet contributed to the rebirth of sacred art in France. [JG]

[137] Louis Le Cardonnel (1862–1936) was an elegiac poet who joined the priesthood. [JG]

[138] Originally from Switzerland, Alexandre Blanchet (1882–1961) went to Paris to become a painter. Returning to his homeland in 1914, he benefited from his great renown and made numerous mural programs for public monuments. [JG]

Many men of God, wakened by defeat[139] and ardent to restore the altar, may call upon a Dusouchet. Yet Blanchet is the one who must be commissioned for the embellishment of civic temples, houses of justice, palaces of glory and altars of the Fatherland.

And since the great Puvis is gone, then let his heir be entrusted to cover one of the desecrated walls of the Panthéon as soon as they bring the remains of the master there.[140]

Jean-Julien Lemordant[141] does not willingly leave the tragic point of Penmarch, and if he pushes further to Quimper, for him it is quite a big trip. He prefers rigorous labor in front of the sea to Parisian negotiations and the "politics of art."

Lemordant knows how to submit to the law of his sensibility without getting carried away by it. No painter is more severe about his work and self-satisfied with such little ease.

---

[139] France's defeat in the Franco-Prussian War of 1871 was the reason for Emperor Napoleon III's downfall and the installation of the Third Republic, which proclaimed the separation of church and state in 1905. [JG]

[140] Puvis de Chavannes, one of the masters of Symbolism, died in 1898. One can admire his murals in the Panthéon, the Sorbonne and the Hôtel de Ville in Paris. The Panthéon (formerly the Church of Sainte-Geneviève) was secularized by the Third Republic. Contrary to Salmon's wish, Puvis de Chavannes' remains were not transferred to this civic temple, where "the grateful Fatherland" pays homage to its great men, but are buried in the old cemetery in Neuilly-sur-Seine. [JG]

[141] Jean-Julien Lemordant (1882–1968) was known for painting a large mural for the Hôtel de l'Épée (of the Sword) in Quimper, Brittany. Seriously injured in his eyes during World War I, he finally regained his sight after several operations. He died accidentally, killed by a tear-gas bomb during the protest marches in the Latin Quarter of Paris in 1968. His scenes of fishing and of fairground entertainers can be found in many French museums (Paris, Quimper, Rennes and Nantes) and in the United States (New York, Yale's museum in New Haven, and Chicago). [JG]

He paints the sea and the people at the sea. The contrast is poignant, because nothing is more tragic than the sea of Penmarch, and all is joy in the adornment of the fishermen and harvesters of the coast—a joy of exotic quality.

"Those from Penmarch," as they say in Quimper, have a variety of tones in their clothes that is Far Eastern in taste, which, truth be told, is of little surprise to these country folk with features like Mongolian magicians.

Jean-Julien Lemordant knew how to not conform to this exoticism excessively. Through the science of lighting, he extracts the right harmony from a barbaric combination of colors, with the somber sea as a screen.

Other canvases demonstrate the adaptability of Jean-Julien Lemordant's talent. After the fishermen and harvesters—who permitted him to realize the powerful and joyous decoration of the Hotel of the Sword in Quimper—he depicted the destitute and derelicts, lamentable downtrodden of the city in a sad procession along a wall, those walls of the prison, the barracks, the hospital and the cemetery, waiting for a loaf of bread (the insulting gift from official charity) and eternal rest.

A third aspect of Lemordant's talent and sensibility is that he still paints *saltimbanques*—those whom one might call riders from the sea. These extraordinary acrobats install their circus of canvas on the beach and gallop nude on their performing horses among the waves while their wives and sisters (tanned mermaids in scarlet rags) make soup and nurse their little ones.

Jean-Julien Lemordant loves them fraternally. Interpreting their tricks or failures, he allies these wanderers with crude sardine-fishermen and peasants whose wrinkles are fertilized by the waves.

When he was a restless and nervous student, Camoin had the good fortune of capturing Cézanne's interest.[142] He met the sublime old man, the peasant

---

[142] Charles Camoin (1875–1965) visited Cézanne in 1901 and became one of his friends and correspondents. In 1905 he exhibited in the Salon d'automne's "Cage aux Fauves" ("Wild Beasts' Cage"). Then he began an international career, exhibiting with Düsseldorf's Sonderbund group at the end of 1910 and in the 1913 International Exhibition of Modern Art (known as the Armory Show) that arrived in New York, Chicago and Boston. [JG]

of genius, whom he was able to get to know and understand so well that he would not slavishly steal from him. Cézanne did not ask Camoin to try to resemble him. The giant of Aix-en-Provence counseled the young man to make studies in the Louvre from the great decorative masters Veronese and Rubens, in the same way one paints from nature. He wrote to him in September 1903: "Couture[143] told his students: 'Be in good company,' meaning: 'Go to the Louvre.' But after having seen the great masters who remain there, one must quickly leave and verify for oneself, through contact with nature, the instincts and sensations of art which reside within us."[144]

Camoin had no trouble following this beneficial advice. He delights in life, but he is a slow man and lazy artist. He developed without rushing himself because it is his nature to enjoy each thing for a very long time, especially when he realizes that he will have to give it up and eventually condemn it. Exquisite cruelty! A bit feline, and the mark of a somewhat feline art. Camoin painted beautiful portraits and suave still-life paintings. He translated our spectacles of Parisian folly in quite an aristocratic manner, while disengaging them from their immediate vulgarity. If he goes far back into the past to find pure secrets, he consults more willingly the Chinese of the divine eras than the Primitives of Flanders or Italy.[145]

Happy with his vigor, Alexandre Urbain[146] is a scrupulous painter. Aware that true audacity is not to invent without moderation, aware as well that one must

---

[143] Thomas Couture (1815–1878) is an artist known for his large history paintings, such as *The Romans of the Decadence,* 1847 (which now belongs to the Musée d'Orsay in Paris). [JG]

[144] A letter from Paul Cézanne in Aix-en-Provence to Charles Camoin, stationed in Aix during his military service, September 13, 1903. Camoin was also a student of Gustave Moreau's, along with Matisse, Marquet, Flandrin and Rouault (Herschel B. Chipp, *Theories of Modern Art* [Berkeley: University of California, 1968], 18). [BGN]

[145] Fifteenth-century Flemish and Italian art. [BGN]

[146] An Alsatian painter, Alexandre Urbain (1875–1953) painted the murals in the Palais de la Découverte in Paris. [JG]

distrust the systematic movement toward the left, he knows it is appropriate, on the contrary, to secure one's personality through a discipline that is nothing other than hygiene for an acknowledged temperament.

In brief, his body of work testifies to a noble effort toward certitude and a moderate classical sentiment. One has played so much with words that it is useful to insist on not believing from these comments that Alexandre Urbain's painting is very boring.[147]

All his canvases are not the same quality, but the artist has indeed understood the sunny grace of the Italian countryside that is so familiar to him.

I believe (and the participation of Urbain in the last salons justifies to me my reasons to believe) that his trip through Italy, despite the richness and abundance, was only a trip for studies—a warming up of the painter's sensibility.

Alexandre Urbain will fully realize himself in front of the clear landscapes of France one day.

Now here are some young artists in the absolute sense.

Let us begin with the Marsellais L.M. Verdilhan[148] who arrived early enough to participate in a few of the Fauves' pitched battles.

L.M. Verdilhan is violent and sentimental. His art bears the mark of his popular and Southern origins. Like that of van Dongen, the talent of this young painter is to a great extent made of proletarian violence, which has no chance of subsiding. But Verdilhan's abundant and frank Southernness is the corrective for that violence—it is justified by a natural alliance that overcomes a fairly rough way of thinking. Moreover, one does not find in the works of this Provençal with primitive instincts that gluttonous amazement, which in the work of a van Dongen wearies us so quickly.

---

[147] Often misused, the word *classique* (classical) has ended up meaning that a work is skillful without any creativity. [JG]

[148] Louis Mathieu Verdilhan (1875–1928) was a Fauve painter influenced by Cézanne, who enjoyed some fame after World War I. [JG]

L.M. Verdilhan, an energumen about emotion, is indifferent to the quality of his most profound anxiety, but he is attractive. His muse is dissolute and poignant; she solicits by stammering unknown prayers; she tries her hand at the worst artifice of the city, but her charm remains perfectly rustic—she speaks both in slang and dialect.

If the artist managed to discipline his virginal strengths, he could occupy a considerable place—the place that van Dongen will never occupy because he is too distant from nature, breathing in the music hall atmosphere of the museum.

L.M. Verdilhan, on the other hand, sees straight ahead like Vincent van Gogh, and this young man from Marseille has understood everything from the best lessons of Cézanne.

Without lowering the tone, he should limit his palette a bit, which is abundant to the point of triviality. Also, he must take care not to confuse line and color—as did Matisse.

Robert Lotiron[149] has already escaped the danger that L.M. Verdilhan must still conquer. Like him, he has a fiery stroke and the gift of impetuous color, but his stronger sanity puts him in a position to choose his own discipline.

Slowly and wisely, Lotiron has learned to construct. One should not chide him for being content with painterly pieces. Lotiron is quite capable of realizing, with brio, a sufficiently worked out picture. But he maintains self-control and knows how to submit his imagination to healthy restraint.

The art of Robert Lotiron originates evidently from the art of Cézanne who teaches him how to contemplate nature with magnificent humility. That is to say, with the respect owed to a perpetually unknown world and the certainty of extracting from it a particle of beauty, no longer nameless but

---

[149] A friend of La Fresnaye, Robert Lotiron (1886–1966) returned to realist figures after a brief flirtation with Cubism. His work belongs to museum collections in Chicago, Los Angeles, Philadelphia, Le Havre and Paris. [JG]

conforming to impulses from the soul and senses. There is the great effort—to achieve exact control of these impulses (sometimes twins and sometimes enemies) in order to keep one's balance.

Naturally impetuous, Robert Lotiron sometimes holds himself back just enough to shock us with a severity in the architecture of his lines, which we feel can't satisfy the most secret desire of the artist—still contradicted by the generosity of his colors. By restraining himself in such a way, he might seem to be too overly a parodist of Cézanne.

We must have confidence in this artist who so often has known how to look at the world with the avid innocence of a child—so amazed that he reaches out to hold it with a still weak but determined hand.

United by a brotherhood of common feelings with the artists of whom we have just spoken, Alfred Lombard[150] is of another race.

Traditional French culture awakens in him a feeling for art, and because his output is not yet considerable (offering few examples to our critic), we have not been able to discover what overriding cause made him choose painting as a means of expression, rather than music or poetry.

With his native faculties, he only tolerates a very direct sensuality which will save him from dandyism, the worst and the surest pest that could have plagued him.

Although he distances himself each day a bit more from Jean Puy, this painter, among his slightly older colleagues, is the one to whom Alfred Lombard is most evidently connected by virtue of his execution and composition.

On the other hand, the quality of his imagination and the intellectual character of his sensibility would bring him, more accurately, closer to Bonnard. How bookish would Alfred Lombard's art be if this artist did not have the

---

[150] Alfred Lombard (1884–1973) exhibited in Paris in 1910, then organized the Salon de Mai in Marseille with Pierre Girieud. After World War I, he worked for La Compagnie Générale Transatlantique. His decorative murals for the ocean liner *Normandie* (1935) are considered masterpieces of decorative art in France from the 1930s. [JG]

good fortune of coming from Marseille! Better than a Parisian (living in a climate more conducive to exclusiveness), the Marseillais has those instants of soul when all souls merge. Then all at once the artist is himself, the mariner of the old port, the proud merchant, the man who returns from the Orient, the talkative cook, and the hooligan.

In fact, tiring of what we called earlier "painterly pieces,"[151] Alfred Lombard aspires to the large canvas. He might have been in too much of a hurry to create it, but his critical intelligence is sharp enough to garner some profit from his own errors.

Of all the horizons, Alfred Lombard prefers that of the sea. The rhythm of the sea gives his canvases their most certain solidity. Very modern, he knows how to situate a nude in a contemporary interior with the sea lighting the windowpanes, and yet he does not resort to the convention of the "model in the studio" or those scenes in the powder room, so tiresome when a Lautrec does not extract from them an ambiguous philosophy.

Impertinence of spirit and dilettantism in form are the last demons that set upon this exceptionally gifted painter, who will from now on know how to conquer them.

Satisfied to be a Fauve, Francis Picabia stretches no further, and as a Fauve, he is a latecomer.[152]

---

[151] An allusion to Robert Lotiron's works, which go further than mere "painterly pieces." [JG]

[152] First an Impressionist, then won over by Fauvism followed by Cubism, Francis Picabia (1876–1953) became, late in life, one of the principal leaders in the New York and Paris Dada movements. In 1913, he exhibited in the Armory Show, and then in 1915 at Stieglitz's little gallery called "291." His various mechanical drawings with esoteric titles made him a major proponent of the avant-garde. In 1912, he was instead considered a "dabbler." [JG]

The discord between his colors and his drawing is complete; the colors break the lines instead of nourishing them, and it is a great shame because Picabia has the real qualities of a draftsman.

However, his fairly assured drawing only let him construct some good, isolated figures; his groups of nudes are not harmonious.

His sense of decoration appears the most cursory and merely attains a slight stylization. Finally, this painter, whom we must consider here because he plays an important role in the groupings of young artists, and because despite his faults he has that quality of being himself, lacks taste way too much in his choice of colors. Besides that, he uses them with enough skill. Still, what a mawkish and splashy combination—and truth to tell, so impoverished—of subdued carmines and violets that are not the result of intelligent, luminous contributions!

Because taste fails him—taste which is the balancing pole—Picabia has been sterile for such a long time, dedicating himself to tedious new beginnings.

Now, I will treat three artists who are quite diverse in value—and yet, it seems reasonable to draw a parallel among them, as they have given rise to the same reproach: I mean André Lhote, Marchand, and R.F.N. de La Fresnaye. On more than one occasion, these young artists have been accused of their excessive taste for archaism and popular prints, which, one asserted, was a misunderstood influence received from Raoul Dufy (an underrated artist) via Friesz. To that reproach, André Lhote replied quite wittily that the reason might be insufficient to make Dufy known at his expense.

Certainly, it would be deplorable that the taste of very seductive old prints alienated several of the most gifted and fervent from "the bitter summits of pure painting."

Let us begin by showing some prudence when we are told about pure painting.

Now, André Lhote, Marchand, R.F.N. de La Fresnaye do not lean toward this end, and we must, after all, acknowledge this is their right. So, why the confusion?

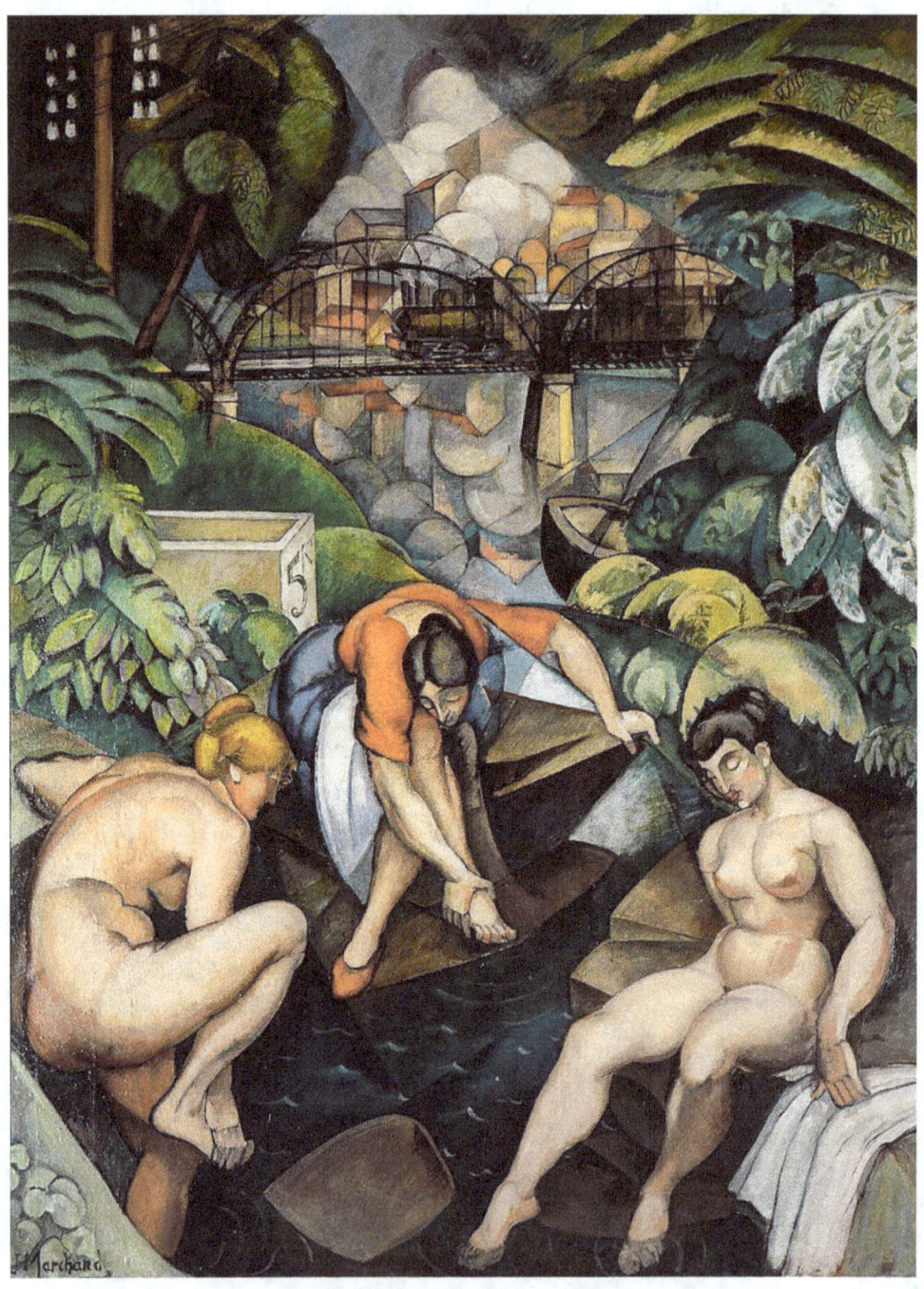

Figure 14. Jean Marchand, *La Source*, 1911

Furthermore, I do not believe that any one of them has been influenced by Dufy. I have already said of the latter that he was a secondary painter and our greatest engraver, a popular printmaker of the first order. Now he is a painter who submits to his own influence as an engraver.

But it does not mean that those who sometimes ask for advice from old printmakers have completely succumbed to the influence of Dufy.

André Lhote[153] has become convinced that the color print sustains painting through direct relationships. This alliance, according to him, satisfies the urgent need to retrieve a certain truly French style, capable of capturing pictorial elements in everyday reality.

Here is how the theories of André Lhote may be summarized, according to his own casual remarks:

"Views of Perspective" quite often copy the pictures of Claude Lorrain. Épinal images[154] and other popular prints reproduce the battles of David, Gros, Vernet, etc. and interpret Poussin; through color and systemization of the model, they revive primitive painters and at the same time often anticipate modern painting, from Matisse to the Cubists.

Great painters, like Brueghel the Elder, possess a rigor supported by drawing, clear tones, popular laxity in poses, and, more generally, a rustic and decided inspiration which are the principal virtues of printmakers.

---

[153] André Lhote (1885–1962) became well known as a painter, theoretician and teacher of Cubism to which he introduced genre scenes. He opened his own academy in 1921 on the rue d'Odessa in Montparnasse. Several of his students became famous in other fields, such as the filmmaker William Klein, the photographer Henri Cartier-Bresson and the singer Serge Gainsbourg. His correspondence with Jean Paulhan (published by Gallimard in 2009) contains precious information about the period from 1919 to 1961. [JG]

[154] Épinal prints were inexpensive reproductions of popular imagery, ranging from copies of fine art paintings to folkloric emblems. The publishing company existed from 1760 to 1914. [BGN]

André Lhote still asserts that such resemblances between color prints and painting are deep and indisputable, but they must not lead to forgetting that the craft of painting has particular demands that would be foolhardy to do without.

At least, the artist has the right to love tender and familiar spectacles to which printmakers gave a nobility more striking than what the Renaissance artists could give to their allegories (which André Lhote thought were bombastic), and to express his fantasy with the unfettered freedom that they enlisted.

It is evident that paying similar attention to anonymous masters liberates, at the very minimum, a Lhote from imitating his contemporaries.

I cannot see what Lhote owes to Carrière (as someone wrote), save for certain general directions.

If he is not a disciple of Dufy, he is (like Marchand and La Fresnaye) a cousin of the Cubists, with whom he shares concerns, because he discovered elements of their discipline in popular art from the past.

But he does not follow them toward the direction of "pure painting." Now, maybe those fine contradictions will give birth to this ideal painting.

Without declaring an eclecticism of bad quality, let us be glad that we still hope to see one day so many artists meet at the crossroads where logically drawn routes must lead.

Defending Marchand[155] is not as easy as defending Lhote. Marchand has liked the image for the image's sake too much and contents himself with that too often.

He has asked too much of popular print artists. He did not restrain himself from seeking in their images what relates to the masters so that, sometimes, they come up to the same level. He claimed to learn from them about naivety.

---

[155] Jean Marchand (1883–1940) started exhibiting in 1910 in Paris and in London, where he attracted the attention of the English critics Roger Fry and Clive Bell. He evolved toward Cubism and participated in the Section d'Or exhibition in 1912. [JG]

However, naivety is a gift—the very gift of childhood! Naivety is forbidden to the civilized person of the twentieth century, and there is some guilty weakness in the cultivated man to play the simpleton. Marchand's figures are too often just good chaps.

This error, which has a firm grasp on the false naivety of the painter, still has another cause.

Marchand—contradicting in this way even his forced naivety—wanted to seek out a new expression for the movement. This preoccupation (common to most modern artists) led to the fortunate deformation, which magnificently rejuvenated French painting, and which insults our conservatives most violently.

But deformation in the manner of Cézanne, Gauguin (and Carrière, too, who religiously blurs the figure with atmosphere), Matisse and Friesz, was not sufficient for Marchand. He went on to imagine the multiplication of figures.

Thus, in one of his most recent canvases, *Plowing*, four figures toil on one single plow. These four people are the same laborer in motion. There is only one plow, you will tell me. Oh my God! It still hasn't responded to one individual effort and a collective representation.

This cinematographic research is rather seductive and not absurd in itself.[156] It would suffice to distinguish Marchand, but the execution still remains somewhat crude.

It is the cult of naivety that gives Marchand the right (which we would not know how to grant him) to be satisfied. This error is his only authentic innocence.

However, Marchand will redeem himself through his gifts as a realist. His initial impression of the landscape (which, without fail, he isn't always able to disguise) is powerful. Love of the tangible universe makes him more obedient than Lhote, who has taken the dangerous trouble of codifying his sensibility.

---

[156] This research became fashionable with the first Futurist exhibition, as is evident in its influence on Marcel Duchamp's *Nude Descending a Staircase*, 1912 (Philadelphia Museum of Art). [JG]

I do not perceive any real link between the art of R.F.N. de La Fresnaye[157] and that of the two aforementioned artists.

However, several people accuse him of being only a popular print artist as well.

R.F.N. de La Fresnaye is instead a decorator.[158] And he even has the gifts of an official decorator; his art is often a civic art. If our authorities had a little less corrupt idea of what must be a republican aesthetic, R.F.N. de La Fresnaye would find a way to decorate the national walls. He would cover them with works that would be full of joy and movement, spring and gladness, worthy of the painter who revealed to us *The Man Drinking and Singing,* the same we had to praise, not long ago, for his shivering *Artillerymen.*

R.F.N. de La Fresnaye is not a popular print artist, because his art is not popular in the narrowest sense of the word—that is to say, a spontaneous art, like the song of the streets or the refrain of a goatherd, a direct expression of primitive feelings.

Neither is R.F.N. de La Fresnaye's manner that of Marchand. Preoccupied, like the latter, with inscribing on the canvas the vibrant arc of movement, he scores his goal not by fixing all the instants of his figures' gestures, but by translating, through a color-induced fantasy, vibrations of the atmosphere.

---

[157] Roger-François-Noël de La Fresnaye (1885–1925) was a student at the Académie Jullian where he became friends with Dunoyer de Segonzac, Lotiron, Boussingault and Albert Moreau. His first paintings are realistic in style, similar to caricatures, and somewhat linked to popular imagery. He then became interested in Picasso's Cubism and the laws of simultaneity promoted by Robert Delaunay. He contracted tuberculosis as a soldier in World War I and was discharged in 1918. His health continued to deteriorate. He abandoned the Cubist style in favor of the return to a modernist classicism. In 1922, he ceased painting and died on November 27, 1925, six years after the Armistice. [JG]

[158] The word "décorateur" in this context means one who paints on walls, such as murals. [BGN]

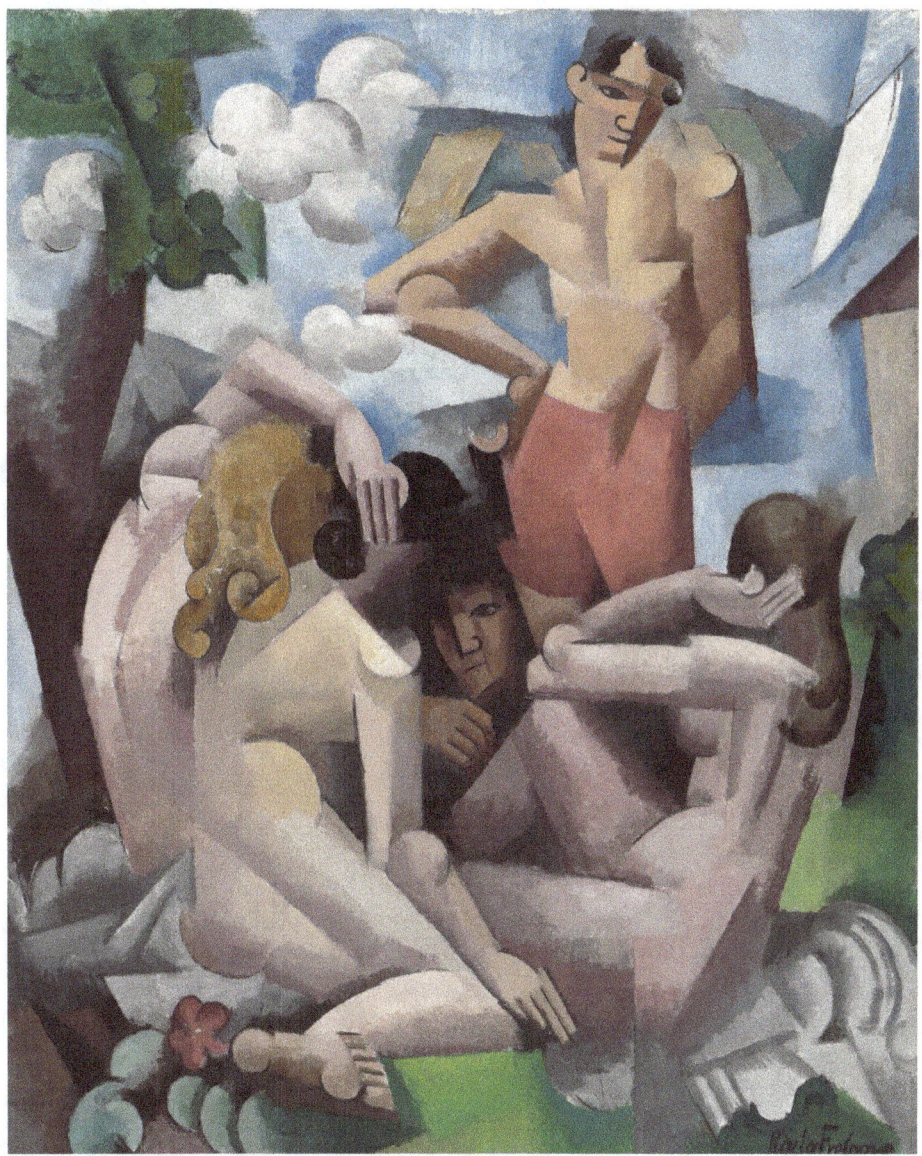

Figure 15. Roger de la Fresnaye, *The Bathers*, 1912
National Gallery of Art, Washington, D.C.

In his *Cuirassier* and his *Artillerymen*,[159] the horses, men and cannons are perfectly immobile, if one isolates them. But the artist does not jail them in

---

[159] *Cuirassier*, 1910–11, Musée National d'Art Moderne, Centre Georges Pompidou, Paris; *Artillery*, 1911, Metropolitan Museum of Art, New York. [BGN]

those clouds of accessory dust which were indispensable for É. Detaille.[160] R.F.N. de La Fresnaye animates his figures through the power of movement that they have created.

Because he needs to translate that, the works of this young painter—our latest military painter—show exceptional qualities of depth. So, we are quickly convinced that the picture on the easel is only a temporary measure for what is intended for the wall.

I already requested that R.F.N. de La Fresnaye paint a wall of a barracks, one in a military academy refectory or the ceiling of a room in the High Council for War at Les Invalides. What minister will want to try this? Have no fear. The walls that the brush could spoil are so humble that we can sacrifice them to this experience.

But the brush of La Fresnaye would not spoil anything; the solicitude of the State would liberate this young artist, who (sooner than the best of those with whom he shares a treasury of fertile ideas) gave to us through new methods, the promise of the composed work.

A painter of limited inspiration, Tobeen[161] celebrates the Basque country through the consecration of the game of pelota, and truly, Tobeen's painting is a *pelotari*'s painting.

---

[160] A painter of military subjects, Édouard Detaille (1848–1912) was considered a *pompier* artist. His most famous work, *Le Rêve* (1888), which Salmon refers to, can be found in the Musée d'Orsay in Paris. [JG]

[161] Félix-Élie Bonnet, known as Tobeen (1880–1938), came from Bordeaux, like André Lhote. In 1907, he visited the artist colony called La Ruche (the beehive) on Passage Dantzig in Paris (15th arrondissement) where he found his first studio. In 1912, he participated in the exhibition La Section d'Or, which was organized by the three brothers Marcel Duchamp, Jacques Villon and Raymond Duchamp-Villon. He was chosen for the Armory Show in 1913 in New York. *Les Pelotaris* (*The Pelota Players*) of 1912 remains his best-known work. In 2012, the Museum of Fine Arts in Bordeaux presented a retrospective of his work entitled *Tobeen, un poète du cubisme*. [JG]

Indeed, we identify in it the work of a man to whom the most familiar horizon is that of the bare white wall struck by the balls of players as beautiful as classical athletes.

His obsession is so great that if Tobeen paints a scene of the harvest, he lends to his peasants, armed with their scythes, the curved arms of the pelota players, and he borrows his colors from all that moves, all that lives in the space inscribed between the two walls: the yellow of the ground and the faces hardened by the glaring light, the white of the stones and the clothes, the blue of the sky and the Basque caps.

To all the action of the crowd, Tobeen gives the particular virtue of a game—a brutal and complicated game. For this very personal artist, life is an eternal pelota match.

Therefore, deformation is not real in his works. The artist chose, once and for all, movements and attitudes without tricks, because both are familiar to him and because each day he discovers them anew.

Has Dunoyer de Segonzac[162] cheated with Cubism? His gifts connect him to some artists who are very distant from the Cubists—and yet their art is going to immobilize and crystallize itself.

Dunoyer de Segonzac has been conscious of this peril and, without submitting himself to the ascetic test that a Metzinger or a Le Fauconnier imposed on themselves, he has applied to traditional painting all that in their research could delay the break in continuity.[163]

---

[162] André Dunoyer de Segonzac (1884–1974), an independent artist best known for his engravings, met Salmon, Max Jacob, Dufy, and Marie Laurencin at the couturier Paul Poiret's salon in 1910. He spent a good part of his life in Saint-Tropez where he bought a house from Camoin in 1925, becoming the writer Colette's neighbor. A film about his life and art was produced by the photographer Michèle Brabo and won a prize during the 1962 Venice Film Festival. [JG]

[163] Dunoyer de Segonzac taught at the Académie de la Palette under Le Fauconnier's direction and alongside Metzinger.[BGN]

His personality proves itself through a variety of subjects. A painter of figures, he seems to aspire to great composition and is close to the Fauves through the violence of his stroke, while borrowing from Picasso's darkest palette.

But, more often and with more happiness, he sets about subjects treated at the same time by Laprade[164] (though he hasn't his virtuosity). However, Dunoyer de Segonzac has more order, more fervent love of the medium and a very deep feeling for luxury in beauty, which makes us think in front of some of his still lifes of those by Fantin-Latour.[165]

A draftsman, he has not managed yet to fix the rhythm of a group. His albums[166] testify to the fact that he is only in pursuit of attitudes, intelligently understood and never absorbed into one anonymous harmony that a great artist ought to subject us to because it carries in it a feeling of the universal.

A disorder of sensations could slow down the maturation of Dunoyer de Segonzac's aristocratic and abundant talent.

For Albert Moreau,[167] the voluptuous is only a pretext for some very austere studies from which we await considerable gains. The art of this young man is profoundly Baudelairian.

If we have attached his name to that of Dunoyer de Segonzac, it is because these two borrow from the same palette. But Cubism, which has not

---

[164] A very fine artist, exhibited at Galerie Larok-Granoff in 2010. See François Roussier, *Pierre Laprade, 1875–1931*, Édition Thalia, 2010. [JG]

[165] Henri Fantin-Latour (1836–1904) is known for the delicacy of his drawing and luminosity in his paintings and pastels. [JG]

[166] In particular, see *Dessins sur les danses d'Isadora Duncan*, La Belle Édition, 1910. [JG]

[167] Luc-Albert Moreau (1882–1948), a good friend of Dunoyer de Segonzac, at first specialized in paintings of places for enjoyment. Seriously wounded in battle in Verdun, he is today considered the best French painter of World War I. [JG]

finished tormenting Dunoyer de Segonzac, never found in Albert Moreau an obedient servant.

André Mare, Dumont, Boussingault, Fontenay, have made some beautiful, promising work.[168] Herbin only discourages us by his too skillful adaptability, but he is a talent.[169]

The Henri Doucet's invention remains discreet, and even timid.[170] The artist only permits himself subtle plays of line. But one can imagine rather soon the emancipation of this painter's gifts, when he ceases to cover canvases on an easel and tackles large decorative paintings on the wall.

Because he owes a lot to Gauguin, Henri Doucet has finally understood that the *pompiers* were right about one point. He no longer scorns inventing a subject.

---

[168] André Mare (1885–1932) devoted himself to decorative art before 1914. Pierre Dumont (1884–1936) was born in Paris and became part of the Rouen School, where he painted the cathedral numerous times. Associated with Marcel Duchamp, Jacques Villon and Francis Picabia, he was also known as an art critic. He founded the revue *La Section d'Or*, an introduction to the famous 1912 exhibition of the same name. Jean-Louis Boussingault (1883–1943) was close to Dunoyer de Segonzac and Luc-Albert Moreau, whom he met at the Académie de la Palette. For notes on Fontenay, look in the previous chapter. [JG]

[169] Auguste Herbin (1882–1960) was part of the Cubist movement from the beginning, exhibiting in the Salon des Indépendants in 1910 alongside Metzinger, Gleize, and Fernand Léger. After that, his work evolved into pure abstraction. [JG]

[170] An excellent portraitist from the Belle Époque, Henri Doucet died at thirty-nine years old on the battlefield during World War I, at the beginning of 1915. [JG] He was a part of the Abbaye de Créteil group, which included Georges Duhamel, Charles Vildrac and Albert Gleizes. He painted a portrait of Duhamel's wife, Blanche Albane, an actress who recited poetry occasionally at the Abbaye soirées. Doucet was also friends with Amedeo Modigliani (1884–1920) and introduced the Italian artist to Dr. Paul Alexandre, his first patron. [BGN]

The oldest landscapes by Henri Doucet show us a beginner smitten with the richness of the medium; little by little, his art is becoming thoughtful, yielding to a more sober and comprehensive harmony.

He takes apart in order to reconstitute, drawing from a value, a volume, a tint, the maximum of intensity, often with moderation and almost always with an emotion that indeed needs to be shared—so evident is the sincerity of his expression.

André Chapuy[171] is a painter of habits—bad habits. This can be attractive if we remember Constantin Guys[172] and Toulouse-Lautrec. But Chapuy knows how to be personal. His technique is sometimes that of the Impressionists whose palette he adopts willingly; however, the feeling of this young artist is like none other. He is the European brother of those Japanese draftsmen who are subtle chroniclers. He paints the life of courtesans—not even the most sumptuous ones. He paints them in bed, at their toilette, and also on their way to wealth or the worst deceptions, which could be translated by one precise word, save for braving too much honesty. Honesty! André Chapuy only violates it gently.

Also a painter of common people, he has added irony to the art of a Raffaëlli,[173] and through this irony, he is influencing the genre for a while. André Chapuy saves us from a pictorial Philippism[174] of the worst kind—

---

[171] André Chapuy (1882–1941) is a painter about whom we know very little. [JG]

[172] Constantin Guys (1802–1892) was known for his drawings, executed in Chinese ink and wash, and in watercolors. Baudelaire's best-known article, "The Painter of Modern Life," published in *Le Figaro* on November 26 and 28 and December 3, 1863, immortalized him. [JG].

[173] A painter and engraver of Italian descent, Jean-François Raffaëlli (1850–1924) was born in Paris and became famous for genre scenes and landscapes located in the Parisian suburbs. He was close to the Impressionists, whom he would meet at the Café Guerbois. [JG]

[174] An allusion to Charles-Louis Philippe, whose novel *Bubu de Montparnasse* (1901) takes place in a neighborhood of prostitutes. See the previous chapter on the Fauves. [JG]

which had been threatening us. An anecdotal artist, he softens the seductive concierge charm that often spoiled Raffaëlli and to which J.K. Huysmans[175] proved himself to be particularly susceptible.

Having only the worry of perfecting himself through discovery and reaching discovery through study, Maurice Asselin[176] is an artist of exceptional sincerity, and he is perhaps of all the representatives of young French painting the one wearied the least by haste. It would be unwise to conclude from this that he dallies.

He was first seduced (without any inconsistency) by Gauguin and Cézanne, Utamaro and Hokusaï. Now the strength of his memories as a passionate admirer of those elected masters allows him to be out of danger when he undertakes realist studies with a fine candor—his choices save him from a fall into the vulgarity of a too direct expression. The flavor of his art is subtle through its singularity, a strong one all the same.

His soul is that of a traveler hardened by fairly difficult stages in a journey so that, as he tells it, the minor setbacks are disregarded. Moved nevertheless by remembering them, he is nourished by that tenderness reserved for important stories.

Maurice Asselin's art seems to me like one of the most susceptible to a high development.

---

[175] The novelist Joris-Karl Huysmans (1845–1906) was first a Naturalist writer, like Émile Zola (1840–1902), and then he supported the Symbolists, such as poet Stéphane Mallarmé (1842–1898) and artist Gustave Moreau (1826–1898). His book *Paris Sketches* (1880) was illustrated with etchings by Jean-Louis Forain and Jean-François Raffaëlli. [JG]

[176] Maurice Asselin (1882–1947) was known above all as a fine watercolorist of the Cornouaille (related to Cornwall in the UK) northwest region of Brittany. See the exhibition catalogue *Maurice Asselin et la Bretagne*, presented by the Museum of Pont-Aven in 2002. [JG]

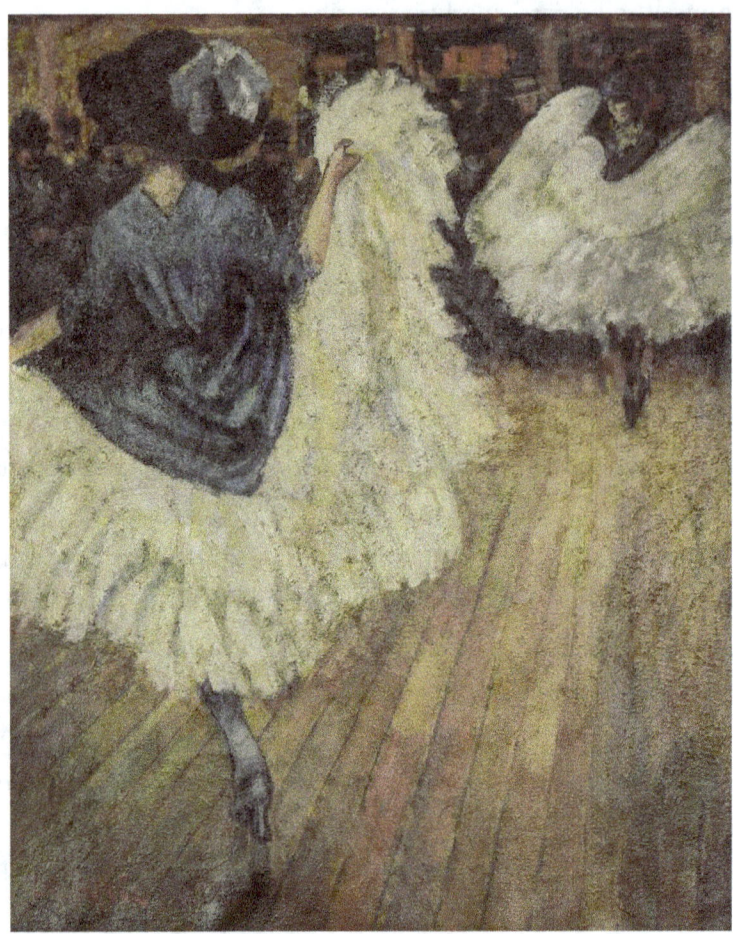

Figure 16. Ludovic-Rodo Pissarro, *French Cancan*, c. 1906
Copyright Stern Pissarro Gallery, London

On the other hand, Ludovic Rodo[177] is only a sensibility expressed nonstop and through all means, without resorting to or straining for effect. Like a lot of sentimental people, nothing attracts him as much as places of debauchery, and in

---

[177] Ludovic-Rodo Pissarro (1878–1962) was the fourth son of the Impressionist Camille Pissarro and is best known in terms of being part of that family. [BGN]

the coarse gesture of a plumed girl dancing the can-can he discovers an innocent pretext. His scenes of public balls do not have the cruelty of Toulouse-Lautrec's works; they are not marked with any sign of lewdness either. Above all, they are valuable for a clear harmony of tones taken from an Impressionist palette.

Ludovic Rodo has benefited from his travels, collecting notes from which he might find material for a rejuvenated work.

Jean Deville,[178] a painter of flowers of all the seasons and a sentimental landscapist, is an artist whom his contemporary Albert André guided at first. Then, without being aware of it, he learned from Henri Matisse the sacrifice of line to color; and yet he demonstrated more logic than the Prince of the Fauves.

Like Dufy, he seems to have one ambition: to be henceforth a decorator. He puts his beautiful ingenious talent to work for industry, the sole resource for an artist who is concerned about saving one of the noblest old French skills from disaster.

I will not finish without conveying my confidence in the future of Challié,[179] nor without naming Jacques Vaillant,[180] a comrade in the study of the most

---

[178] Jean Deville, born in 1872, remains rather obscure. His *Portrait of Nietzsche*, exhibited in 1908 at the Salon de la Nationale, received recognition. Like Dufy, he was tempted to direct his talents as a wood engraver toward industrial production of printed fabric. There is no trace of his work after 1926. [JG]

[179] Jean-Laurent Buffet (1889–1943), called Challié, was the brother of Gabrielle Buffet, who married Francis Picabia. Poisoned by gas in 1915, he spent the rest of his life in his native Jura, distancing himself from the art world. [JG]

[180] Jacques Vaillant took over van Dongen's studio in the Bateau-Lavoir and was part of *la bande à Picasso* (Picasso's Gang). He boasted that he inherited Gauguin's walking stick. See Salmon's chapter "Gauguin's Walking Stick" in *Souvenirs sans fin* (Gallimard, 2004). He made numerous landscapes of Brittany, similar to his friend Maurice Asselin, and then felt he had failed in life and work. Born in 1879, he ended his days in 1934 with a self-inflicted gunshot. [JG]

undisputed Fauves, and who, tempted by all trends, remains faithful to traditional art.

Maybe destiny is not blind for assigning him this role. And when the time of abrupt surprises is over, paid for by such painful and tragic ordeals, perhaps then Jacques Vaillant—a distinguished talent, having played his role well as the guardian of tradition, equally disdainful of Cubism and *pompierism*—will be a lot less distant than he is today from those of his generation for whom the impossible will not impose defeat.

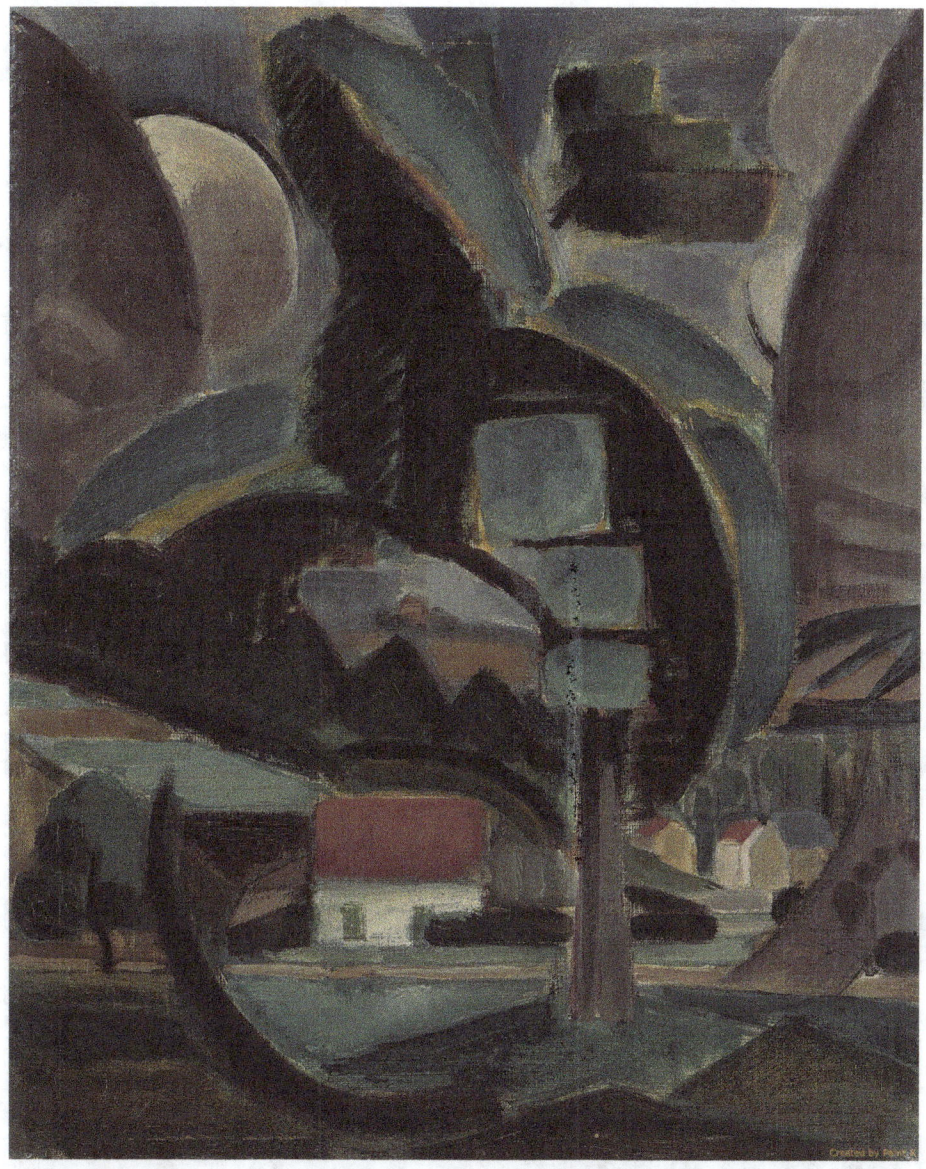

Figure 17. Henri Le Fauconnier, *The Tree*, 1912,
Frans Hals Museum, Haarlem.

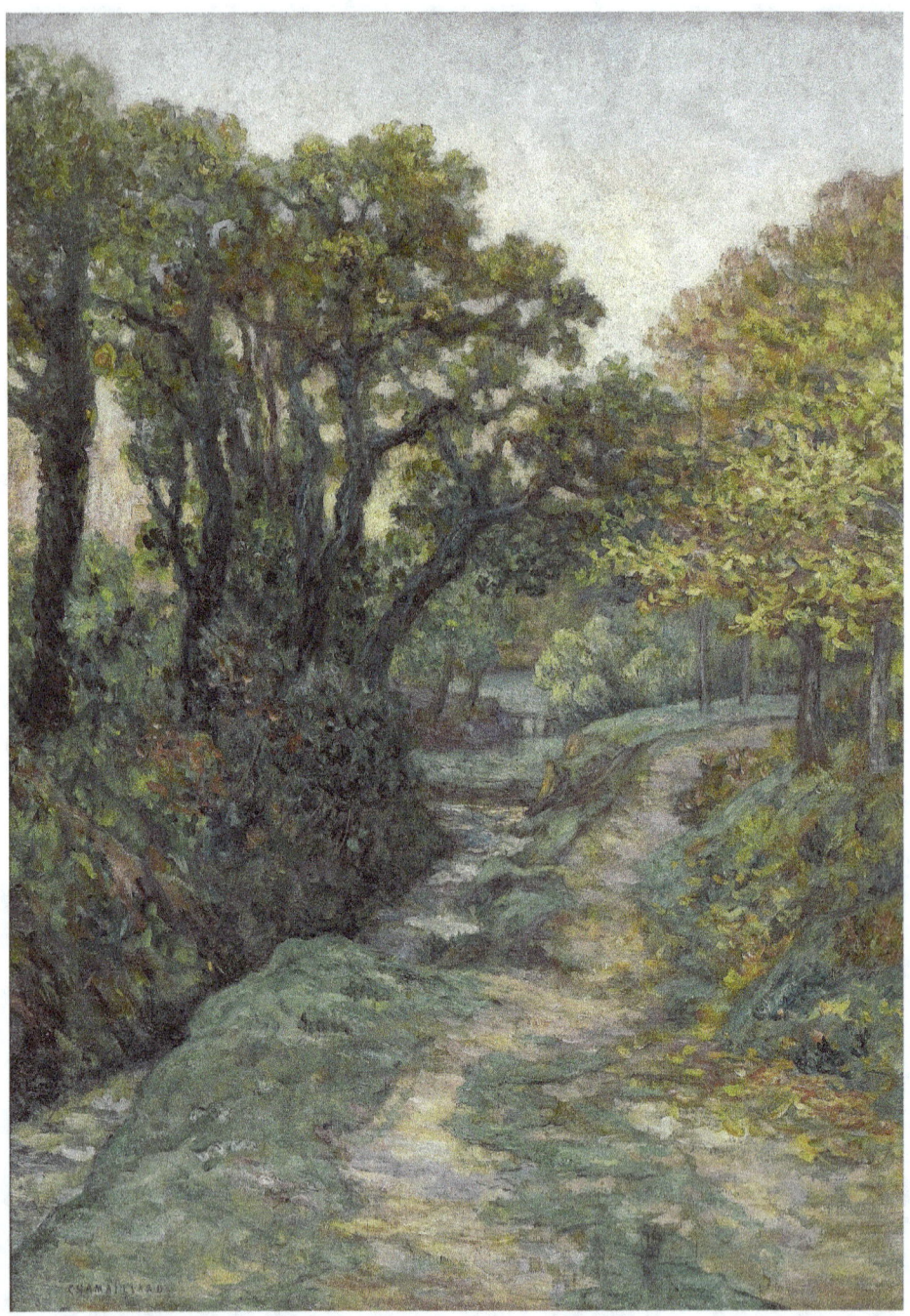

Figure 18. Ernest Ponthier de Chamaillard,
Le Chemin Creu Près du Ruisseau, n.d.

4

A Rebirth of French Landscape Painting

Disgusted by Impressionism, the Fauves, and after them the Cubists, gave little thought to nature.

However, the last revolutionaries, freed from dogmatic trials, no longer feared landscape painting as much.

Albert Gleizes is, I think, the sincerest naturalist among the Cubists. Jean Metzinger, who resorts to natural accessories, deforms them according to his imagination. Robert Delaunay likes water and flowers only when they are imprisoned by the city, and Le Fauconnier turns to the masters of Italy for the secret of his rustic motifs.

And yet, we are witnessing the rebirth of French landscape painting, undertaken by such painters as Charles Lacoste, Louis Charlot, Bausil, Roustan, Deville, and Chamaillard (who began to paint so late in life that we must firmly classify him among the young).

These painters owe nothing to Impressionism; the most timid are forgetting Cézanne. They look directly and re-create with an admirable candor that is not crude.

A frivolous observer might readily take them for the least intellectual of modern artists. He would be making a serious mistake. They are cerebral artists for the same reason as a Picasso, a Matisse, a Friesz, a van Dongen concerned themselves with an art corresponding to modern thought. One of the most profound feelings of our epoch comes from an order that is both moral and social. It is one of those feelings born out of an individualism delivered from its criminal directions.[181] The regionalist feeling (in one word) is an agent of order, reason and beauty, capable indeed of bringing about a revolution all the more stupendous since it will have to sweep away the monuments of three previous revolutions that were generous but corrupted by false passion.[182]

The twentieth-century painters of the soil certainly smack of it more than a Millet, for example, who quickly abandoned his Cotentin and rarely extracted its particular essence.[183] The works of Charlot or Lacoste have more of a genuine flavor. That is because these painters are consumed by a love of their native land. A love we must rediscover after having forgotten it for a

---

[181] Regionalism in France (Basque, Corsican, Breton) has often embraced terrorist activities that are still practiced by the separatist movement in Corsica. Sometimes the police deliberately connected autonomist bombings with those of the anarchists in order to further justify repressive tactics. [JG]

[182] Here Salmon condemns those who try to impose on the artists' so-called universal values, which would limit creative freedom and would not be better than the academic artists' canons. The three revolutions which he refers to may be Impressionism, Fauvism and Cubism, which should not end up as a new way to promote conformity in art. [JG].

[183] Jean-François Millet (1814–1875) is one of the Barbizon masters, known for their landscape paintings. His famous *Angelus* of 1857 (Musée d'Orsay) was imitated so often that it quickly became cliché. Hence there is van Gogh's copy and Salvador Dalí's "paranoiac-critical" appropriation of the work. [JG]

while—the suicide of the small hometown. The salvation of France and art (which we must applaud) is promised to us through the reopening of the provincial studios, which have been closed for a long time.[184]

Charles Lacoste,[185] a painter from the Pyrenees, could be accused of being a bit austere. Despite appearances, it does not interfere at length with the emotion that emanates from his canvases, these panoramic works in which one of the least debatable distinctions is their logical and sober composition. Recently invited to judge the art of Charles Lacoste, Francis Jammes[186] responded by sending a poem. As a matter of fact, lyricism bursts forth, like pure water from

---

[184] Salmon is prescient here as he endorses the return to landscape in modernist terms as the "salvation of France and art." This "return" in the wake of World War I and during the Great Depression is analyzed by Romy Golan in *Modernity and Nostalgia: Art and Politics in France between the Wars* (Yale University Press, 1995). [BGN] This involves, above all, a fidelity to the native soil, a very French notion, much in evidence in the culinary arts in order to protect the quality and flavor of regional products. Here Salmon means that a certain light, which each painter is predisposed to, comes from each "little fatherland," and gives everyone a particular way of seeing. Therefore, when Salmon writes in the chapter "The Fauves" that Poussin could see in Rome the Andelys and thus was making an original painting, it is because this master remained faithful to himself and did not Italianize his work. At that time, when Paris had become the arts capital in Europe, Salmon asked for decentralization to maintain creative diversity in France. This idea continues to succeed today through the opening of two large museums in Metz and Lens, and in local exhibition spaces, such as the André Malraux Museum in Le Havre, which was celebrated with a huge public response. [JG]

[185] Charles Lacoste (1870–1959) studied in Bordeaux where he met the poet Francis Jammes. One can find his landscapes, imbued with spirituality, in the regional museums in Pau and in Bordeaux, and also in the Musée d'Orsay in Paris. [JG]

[186] Francis Jammes (1868–1938) was a famous poet in France, known for his bucolic and humanistic inspiration. His faithfulness to his native soil in the Pyrenees did no harm to his reputation—in fact, to the contrary. [JG]

hard rock, from these landscapes with a vigor that one must learn to cherish, just as one must learn how to strike the rock.[187]

The Pyrenees' natural scenery is a display of warlike and, above all, mystical forms: Peaks stand erect and are grouped like citadels to protect a miracle. Lacoste tries to paint truthfully while translating the landscape's spiritual feeling. "The calm" (such an obsession among contemporary artists that they have altered the word a bit and added it to the slang of the studios) is natural to this painter who gets it without looking for it, because he possesses it in himself. This calm is just right for the integration of forms. In this religious meditation—the sole valid artistic state—nature reveals to us the deep and pure foundations of its harmonies, the mysterious links that unite its elements of vision, line and color. Let us listen to Charles Lacoste himself: "As for the modern anxiety over the decorative,[188] one could find profound reason in the way nature herself appears to our eyes."[189]

Lacoste's alleged austerity is no less deniable than the coldness of the first Cubists. All that touches us henceforth teaches us anew about the art of constructing and is constructed to last. The modern landscapist, as soon as he looks at nature and before he even picks up his brush, pronounces the condemnation of Impressionism to which, after all, we are indebted only for

---

[187] An allusion to the biblical scene when Moses strikes the rock with his staff and water pours forth in the desert. [JG]

[188] Here, the term *décoratif* (decorative art) is not pejorative, but denotes an issue considered among modern painters in order to supersede the limits of easel painting and "decorate" the walls in public buildings. This ambition was recognized and encouraged by Salmon in the preceding chapter "Living Art" wherein he suggests official commissions for the young painters. It gave birth to a number of masterpieces in the twentieth century— from the overture curtain for the ballet *Parade*, which debuted on May 18, 1917, at the Théâtre du Chatelet in Paris ("story" by Jean Cocteau, music by Erik Satie, costumes and set design by Picasso) to the ceiling of the Paris Opéra, painted by Chagall in 1964 in response to a commission by André Malraux, then the Minister of Culture under General de Gaulle. [JG]

[189] Lacoste refers to that impression we have of living in a natural setting as backdrop, with decorative elements such as the clouds, sea, mountains or starry night. [JG]

a more fortunate choice of colors. In Lacoste's case, for example, the concentrated effort of the artist reassembles scattered planes, and the eye chooses the essential. Thus landscape—and all vision, even the imaginative kind (provided it depends on previous direct observations)—shows this unity due to an impression of strength or softness, in accordance with the day and the angle. The soul gives it its absolute meaning.

More unpolished, Louis Charlot,[190] has some fairly rare distinctions. He has given his love completely to his native Morvan. Louis Charlot's work is enjoyable. This painter is not a bold smasher of lines. Although he thinks sometimes about Cézanne, he seeks out parts of his personality while looking at nature with virgin eyes.

From the first snows to the slow thaw, Louis Charlot tells us in the most perfect way about his love of his harsh and peaceful native land—all the dramatic aspects of a valley in winter which will soon delight in the joy of spring promises. Courageously, Louis Charlot rejected all the bad Impressionist lessons, and, although hardly anxious about flashy innovations, he is linked through his drawing to very bold modern painters. Because everything is connected here, we only wanted, and were only able, to concern ourselves in this study with those worthy of being called "men of our time."

In some pictures, inappropriate and too conspicuous figures (a fault that Lacoste would not commit) spoil pure landscapes. Due to a vain concern for the picturesque, these arbitrarily placed figures throw the whole composition off balance. However, little by little, Louis Charlot rejects such errors. The destiny of the modern landscapist, of the regional painter, is rather proud! He

---

[190] Christened "the Painter from Morvan," Louis Charlot (1878–1951) experienced great success beginning in 1920. The most famous among his works is *Les Paysans attablés* (*Peasants Seated at the Table*), from 1913 (Musée d'Autun), based on Le Nain's subjects in Cézanne's style, which earned him Apollinaire's praise as "the Cézannien painter of Peasants." His works have been acquired overseas in such places as Japan, Argentina and the United States. [JG]

has to restore for us the healthy and deep reality of our provinces that were odiously disfigured by functionary painters, academic centralists. Greater artists will collect these scattered elements.[191] They will also remember the wonderful example of application imparted by the best Fauves or Cubists who are by no means revolutionaries but revisers of pictorial values;[192] and then we will have a triumphant French school.

Belatedly rescued by Gauguin from bureaucratic paperwork, Chamaillard is not a student of the master from Tahiti.[193] He simply had the good fortune of learning the painter's craft under a more favorable direction than so many others from that time. In particular, he escaped the influence of Maurice Denis who held court at Pont-Aven. A Breton from Finistère, Chamaillard uncovers Brittany. He paints it in its true colors, which are clear and joyous.

---

[191] Salmon affirms his conviction that each creative person contributes to the birth of a golden age by bringing a stone to the edifice of the future. All the "young" artists who are of their time and have not come to terms with academicism, even if they are not destined for immortality, must be acknowledged. We need many so-called minor painters to enjoy one Picasso and many mediocre attempts before a Douanier Rousseau (one per century) imposes his achievement. Without the faith of these believers, devoted to their art, there would be no chance of miracles occurring one day. [JG]

[192] In the newspapers, and all the way to the Chambre des Députés, the Cubists were accused of destroying the values of French art. Salmon affirms that they are renewing and prolonging them by taking part in a very old tradition, which has nothing to do with the academicism of the École des Beaux-Arts. [JG]

[193] Ernest Henri Ponthier de Chamaillard (1862–1931) met Paul Gauguin in Pont-Aven in 1888 and became a part-time artist with Gauguin's guidance. An amateur artist then, he gave up his career as a lawyer to pursue art full time for a while and then discovered that he was not able to make a living from his art. At the age of fifty in 1912, he was living in Paris and supporting himself as a law clerk while exhibiting occasionally. So he was young in terms of his career, which he started late in life. [BGN]

His work expresses magnificently the joy of the civilized person fascinated by the fresh treasures of rusticity. What a pity that he is not such a young man that we might study him further.

A Catalan from France, joyously independent and devoted to serious labor, like those of his race, Louis Bausil[194] need not regret having endured Impressionist domination during his training. However, we must praise him for his emancipation. It permits him to construct with a rigor that his bold color is indebted to for all its balance. Louis Bausil paints landscapes of the Balearic Islands and, above all, pictures of his Roussillon, very faithfully rendered, which, because of their organization, make us think inevitably of the landscapes of the primitives.[195] His palette has dazzling youthfulness—abundant, luminous and never vulgar. The artist has indeed understood that the Impressionists' search for clarity led to an abuse of whites as artificial and harmful as the bitumen and gravy of the preceding school. He dares admirable combinations of ochre, carmine, cobalt and greens.

---

[194] Louis Bausil (1876–1945) enjoyed a reputation that hardly extended past the borders of Carcassonne and Perpignan, two cities in his native Roussillon, situated in the Vaucluse, a department of southeastern France. [JG]

[195] *Primitifs* in this context refers to fifteenth-century European painting, e.g., French, Flemish and Italian, as we find in Charles Morice statement, quoted in chapter "Les Fauves," p. 22 (in the original). [BGN]

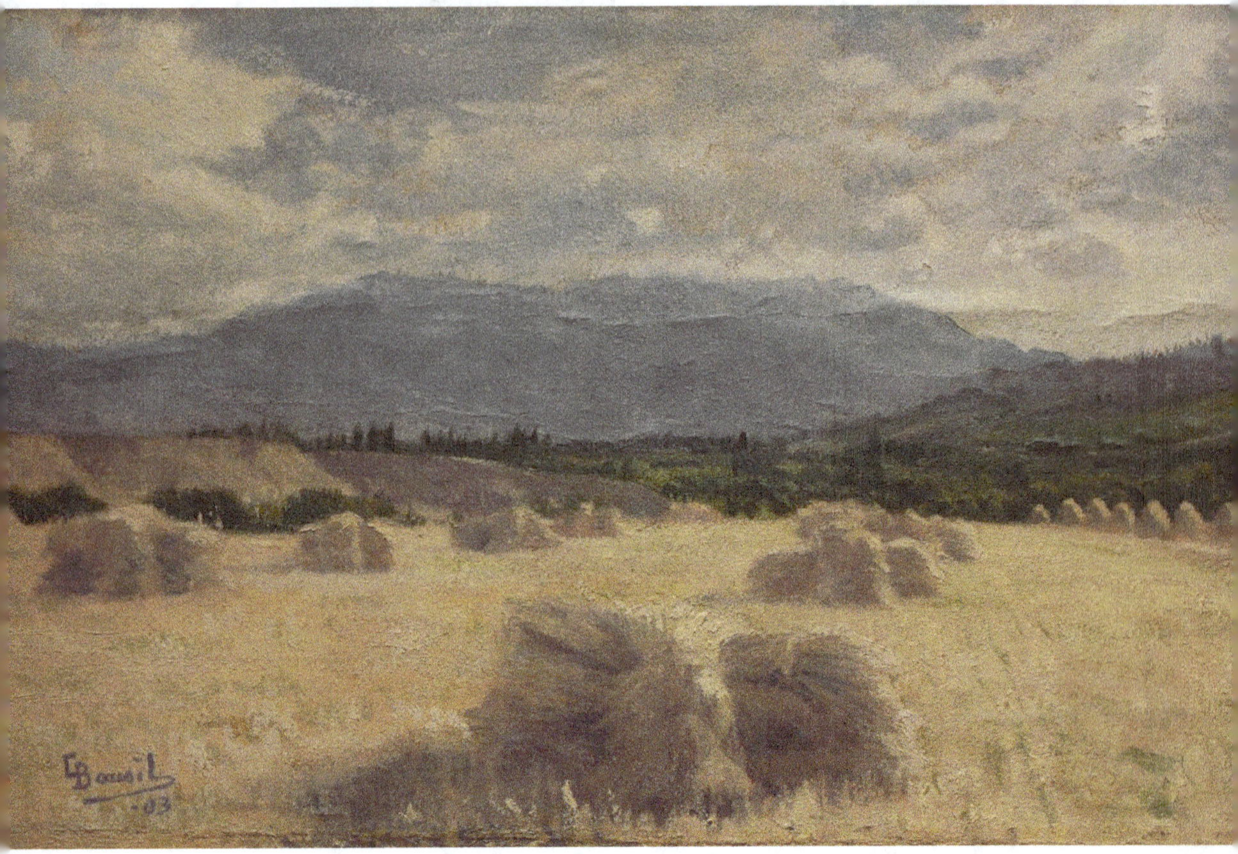

Figure 19. Louis Bausil, *Wheat Field in Cerdagne*, 1903
Musée Hyacinth-Rigaud, Perpignan

A painter of the Forez, Émile Roustan[196] took lessons only from trees, mountains, and powerful, harsh, and yet so radiant springs—wet nurses of its peasant ancestors. He loves and understands a brilliant and crude nature, violent in its essence, yet quelled by the tenderness of the air. Exceptionally

---

[196] Very little is known at this time about Émile Roustan (1877–1945) and his work. Born in Phnom Penh, he left Cambodia at the end of the nineteenth century and settled in Forez, a mountainous region in the Massif Central. [JG]

sensitive to atmospheric variations, Roustan finds in morning fog the virtues of a dazzling spectacle of total light. Truly rustic, he is never clumsy, and I dare to write that this landscapist is a noble realist.

It has been said of Francis Jourdain that he was a Parisian grandnephew of Saint Francis of Assisi.[197] Here a Parisian means a man from the Ile-de-France, like those poets: Gérard de Nerval and Paul Fort.[198] He humanely and religiously loves nature, and it seems that nature always makes herself beautiful to receive him. Beautiful in her everyday dress, both humble and splendid, having been embroidered by the seasons, made golden by the light, washed by the rain, and then shaken by a storm that failed to tear it apart. Francis Jourdain does not seek out the furbelows of the land where frivolous nature is always in holiday dress. He wants her happy, singing and productive, like a laundress from Senlis or Sannois. If opulence seduces him for a moment, he takes refuge in a warm interior and paints two nude women playing with

---

[197] An activist and committed Leftist, Francis Jourdain (1876–1958) was the son of architect, art critic and writer Frantz Jourdain (1847–1935), founder and president of the Salon d'automne in 1903, known for designing the second building of the department store Samaritaine (1903 to 1907) and renovating the first in 1910. Francis Jourdain was the friend of the novelist Charles-Louis Philippe (see Chapter 1 "The Fauves"). A painter, engraver and ceramicist, Jourdain stopped painting in 1911 and turned his attention to the decorative arts. He specialized in making furniture. Beginning in 1913, he invented multifunctional, "interchangeable furniture," made from rearranging basic parts that were manufactured in a series and offered at a low price. He was encouraged by Charles-Édouard Jeanneret (Le Corbusier, 1887–1965) and collaborated with Robert Mallet-Stevens (1886–1945). His autobiography *Né en 76* (*Born in '76*) was published in 1951 (Édition du Pavillon, Paris). [JG]

[198] The Ile-de-France extends around Paris in a circle that is about 30 kilometers (18.6 miles). The cities Senlis and Sannois are part of this region. They were extolled by the poets Gérard de Nerval (1808–1855) and Paul Fort (1872–1960). Nerval was one of the fathers of Symbolism, along with Charles Baudelaire (1821–1867) and Arthur Rimbaud (1854–1891). Paul Fort is known for his *Ballades françaises* (*French Ballads*), which celebrate the charms of his native land. [JG]

a bit of fabric. From this silky rag, he creates richness itself. But Jourdain is truly great as a landscapist whose works are simply gentle and straightforward, abundant in loveliness. An enthusiastic and generous painter, he works with all the more exhilaration because, with his reflective mind, he is in control of his joy.

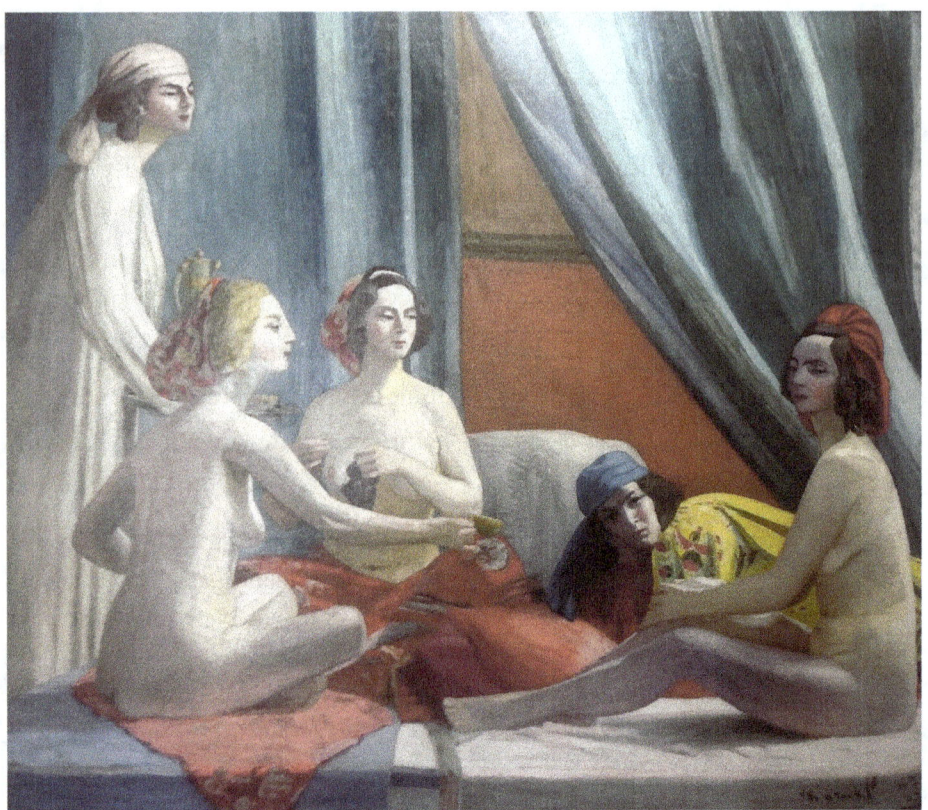

Figure 20. Jacqueline Marval, *Les Odalisques*, 1902-3, Musée de Grenoble

5

Women Painters in the Twentieth Century

Two artists require our attention; they will remain the only unofficial leaders among women artists at the beginning of the twentieth century. One is still attached to a fairly traditional art. The other is inclined to follow the audacious artists of her generation, so that some have gone as far as calling her (very inaccurately in my opinion) the "Muse of Cubism."[199]

---

[199] Guillaume Apollinaire met Marie Laurencin in 1907 and continued his relationship with her until 1912. He reviewed her work for the first time in his critique of the 1908 Salon des Indépendants. In his review of women painters for *Le Petit Bleu*, April 5, 1912, Apollinaire noted that Marie Laurencin participated in two art movements, Fauvism and Cubism, and in a catalogue for her recent exhibition, Fernand Fleuret called her "Our Lady of Cubism." (Apollinaire, *Apollinaire on Art*, 229.) After Salmon finished *La Jeune Peinture française*, Apollinaire included Marie Laurencin among the Cubists in several contexts, including his article "Cubism," *L'Intermédiaire des chercheurs et des curieux*, October 10, 1912, and Méditations esthétiques: Les peintres cubistes (Paris: Eugène Figuière, 1913). [BGN]

I am referring here to Mrs. Marval and Miss Marie Laurencin.[200]

One might readily imagine Mrs. Marval as the queen of a chimerical realm that is populated only by maidens and budding young girls.[201] As sovereign, she would walk through the paths, around the lawns and ponds, in the shadow of a fanciful parasol embellished by the flight of various birds and the blossoming of roses.

No doubt she would share her garden flowers with her subjects, the young girls, the friends of Adrienne and Sylvie.[202]

Mrs. Marval is only a princess of art, and that is enough. If she must buy her flowers from the flower girl who sells them indiscriminately to the artist,

---

[200] The use of Mrs. and Miss preceding the name of a female painter was at the time the correct form. Therefore, for a male artist one would say only Georges Braque or Braque and for a female artist one had to say Miss Marie Laurencin or Miss Laurencin. Today, we should consider this practice discriminatory. [JG]

[201] Jacqueline Marval (née Marie-Joséphine Vallet (1866–1932) was born in Grenoble, the daughter of an amateur musician and artist. She began to paint under the name Marie Jacques in 1884. In 1886 she married Albert Valentin, a traveling salesman, and in 1891 her marriage ended after the death of their infant son. In 1895 she went to Paris and moved in with the painter Jules Flandrin. She met Matisse, Marquet and Rouault through Flandrin, all students at Gustave Moreau's studio. In 1900 she began to call herself Jacqueline Marval. She exhibited at the Salon des Indépendants, Berthe Weill's gallery and in the 1913 New York Armory Show. In 1917 she moved into 19 Quai Saint Michel, where Matisse lived from 1899 to 1908—Marquet took over Matisse's apartment (Gillian Perry, *Women Artists and the Parisian Avant-Garde* [New York: St. Martin's Press, 1995], 156–157; John Elderfield, *Henri Matisse: A Retrospective* [New York: Museum of Modern Art, 1992], 85, 180). [BGN] See the monograph by François Roussier, *Marval 1866–1932* (Édition Thalia, 2008). [JG]

[202] Gérard de Nerval's novella *Sylvie: Souvenirs du Valois* tells about his love for two young girls: Sylvie and Adrienne. *Sylvie* is included in his collection *Les Filles du Feu* (1854). [BGN]

the financier, the *grisette*[203] and the widower, she certainly knows how to compose them in fairy-tale bouquets.

Do you remember the exquisite passage by the beloved Gérard?

"I had hardly noticed, in the ring in which we were dancing, a tall and beautiful blonde, who was known as Adrienne. All of a sudden, following the rules of the dance, Adrienne found herself all alone with me in the middle of the circle."[204]

Mrs. Marval painted that scene excluding the poet himself:[205] Adrienne after the dance, blonde and beautiful in her white dress, is surrounded by her happy companions, chaste and destined to delight virgins. Then, she sings "one of those old ballads full of melancholy and love." Further on, Gérard de Nerval says: "We thought we were in paradise."[206]

We still think so in front of Mrs. Marval's work.[207] She nearly spoiled it with a few excesses of color. Who knows? Perhaps, paradise is not perfect.

Sincerely and loyally, down the paths of fantasy, Mrs. Marval has known how to pursue her work with such logic that today the sequence constitutes a harmonious curve.

This artist with natural gifts is no less a poet than a painter; yet she quite clearly is a painter.

---

[203] An independent working woman, usually a shopgirl or seamstress, a *grisette* pursued liaisons with bohemian types, such as writers, artists and musicians. She was considered a woman of easy virtue, but not a prostitute or courtesan. [JG]

[204] Part 2 of *Sylvie,* entitled "Adrienne," third paragraph. [BGN]

[205] Jacqueline Marval painted a picture entitled *Fantaisie sur Sylvie,* known also as *Le Chant d'Adrienne* and *Hommage à Gérard de Nerval* (1910–1911). It was part of her first solo exhibition at Galerie Druet in 1912. [BGN]

[206] Ibid., fourth paragraph. This quotation from *Sylvie* can be found in all the textbooks on French literature used by high school students. [JG]

[207] For more information on Jacqueline Marval, visit: https://www.jacqueline-marval.com/ and see the article by Beth S. Gersh-Nešić on Jacqueline Marval, in *Bonjour Paris,* April 7, 2020, online. [BGN]

The painter-poets are good workers if they are poets of quality. If the brushstroke of a Rochegrosse[208] is mediocre and vulgar, that is because his imagination is worthless.

One of Mrs. Marval's great distinctions—the kind of distinctions that create talent—is having known how to control her fantasy without constraining it.

The characters born from her verve are so numerous a crowd that the artist can calmly and strictly choose her favorites.

Mrs. Marval was criticized for being mannered, artificial and affected by I don't know what kind of perversity. That's not entirely accurate.[209]

Sensuality does not need innate brutality in order to remain healthy; it deserves to be honored, even if it is spiced by the well-thought-out charms of a premeditated artifice.

Anyway, modern ideas on love, sensuality and modesty are generally absurd.

Yet, what offends some in the work of this artist (who, despite such critiques, prevails) has the opposite effect of comforting me, as a wonderful artistic spectacle that is fed with sufficiently deep feelings to produce a perfectly genuine emotion.

⚜

By virtue of her boldness, Miss Marie Laurencin[210] is indeed worthy of participating in public displays of innovative artists. She is their muse, despite herself.

---

[208] Georges-Antoine Rochegrosse, stepson of the poet Théodore de Banville, student of Gustave Boulanger and Jules Lefèbvre, an academic and Orientalist of the late nineteenth and early twentieth centuries. [BGN]

[209] Marval was considered an eccentric because of her affected way of dressing. Her hair was dyed blue or green, which created quite a stir at the time of the artistic soirées. [JG]

[210] Two biographies on Marie Laurencin are recommended, one by Flora Groult (Mercure de France, 1987) and the other by Bertrand Meyer-Stabley (Pygmalion, 2011), as well as the exhibition catalogue for *Marie Laurencin (1883–1956)*, curated by Daniel Marchesseau, published by the Musée Marmottan Monet and Éditions Hazan, 2013. [JG]

A rigorous technique and certain austerity of lines link her to them. But she is greatly alien to them in terms of imagination since the Cubists still repudiate it. In fact, the subjects in their "pictures" are mere allegories.[211] Thus, they resemble, despite themselves, the Parnassian poets who used to banish inspiration.[212]

To paint her Diana-huntresses riding on does impishly mounted on little wheels, her tender Amazons, and her seemingly learned Nymphs, the artist had no other model but herself. Several of today's young poets appear in her works too, even though they didn't actually pose in front of her.[213]

Miss Marie Laurencin is one of the rare painters of today capable of illustrating a poem without betraying the idea of the poet.

When the young artist composes according to her own inspiration, everything is not always clear in her works. But the abstruse is also part of our tradition.

Miss Laurencin is a painter of grace. Too subtle to be simple (simplicity is not particularly admirable), she is gifted enough in her feeling for moderation not to be mannered.

It would be wrong to believe her inspiration is bookish; she has all the poet's emotions, but she is a painter above all else. She composes diligently but freely, because the transposition occurs naturally in her mind even before she has picked up her brushes.

---

[211] Salmon means that the fragmented objects are represented by intelligible signs (for example, the strings of the violin or the neck of a guitar) which can be identified based on reality and not imagined by the public. As for the painting itself, it refers to the Cubist aesthetic which demonstrates that "the conceptual supersedes the visual." (André Salmon, *L'Art vivant*, G. Crès, Paris, 1920, and other critiques.) [JG]

[212] The Parnassian poets (Théophile Gautier, Leconte de Lisle, etc.), reacting against Romanticism, affirmed the superiority of form over sentimental expression. Their similarity to the Cubists ends there. Their concern for structure did nothing for innovation, whereas the Cubists, by fragmenting objects, representing multiple points of view, and creating collage, never ceased to invent unprecedented plastic solutions. [JG]

[213] Marie Laurencin, *Diana of the Hunt*, 1908, Marie Laurencin Museum, Nagano-Ken, Japan; *Apollinaire and his Friends*, 1909, Centre Georges Pompidou, Musée National d'art moderne, Paris; *Group of Artists*, 1908, Baltimore Museum of Art.

Miss Marie Laurencin's fantasy belongs to no one; she does not come from that Munich which welcomed the dreams of Tehran.[214]

This young girl, with her innocent and deep eyes, has looked at the museum just like she observes nature. Therein lies the great charm of her talent, but that is not the only secret of her art.

The does that populate the gardens in which her fantasy delights may strangely resemble the bronze animals made by the old artists of China, but Miss Marie Laurencin manages to forget, very sincerely. Everything she sees, she makes her own. On the other hand, no one up to now has been able to steal from her what truly belongs to her.

She has probably meditated on the words of Diderot: "Imagine in a pile at your feet, all the trappings of a European man: these stockings, these shoes, these knickers, this jacket, this coat, this hat, this collar, these garters, this shirt—a mere thrift shop. Whereas the trappings of one woman would stock an entire boutique." However, she does not adopt the conclusion of the philosopher: "Skin is nature's clothing."[215]

Her characters are dressed up according to their peculiarly human characteristics, despite even the sometimes arbitrary role that she assigns to them in her compositions.

I had the distinct honor of appearing in one of Miss Marie Laurencin's most seductive compositions. With long hair, I was draped in a flowing blue linen gown that I should like to have the gracious courage to wear in public.[216]

---

[214] There was an exhibition of Islamic art in Munich in fall 1910. Matisse, Marquet and Purrmann are known to have seen it (John Elderfield, *Henri Matisse: A Retrospective* [New York: Museum of Modern Art, 1992], 183). [BGN]

[215] Denis Diderot, "Salon de 1767," in *Salons*, volume III, edited by Jean Seznec and Jean Adhémar (Oxford: Clarendon Press, 1963), 219. [BNG] Here Salmon points out that there are practically no nudes in Laurencin's paintings. [JG]

[216] Marie Laurencin, *André Salmon and his Court*, 1910, Marie Laurencin Museum, Nagano-Ken, Japan. [BGN] In "Nymphes de la Seine," chapter 20 in *Propos d'atelier*, Paris: Crès, 1922, p. 264, Salmon mentions once more the "beautiful blue tunic" that Marie Laurencin lent him. [JG]

But a scientific appetite (which offers nothing positive, if it has allowed this young woman to make pleasant mistakes) has made her rely, with a bit too determined curiosity, on the disheartening work of Picasso. A few attempts lead us to think that Miss Marie Laurencin has nothing to gain from it.[217]

She does not need outside suggestions. Does she remember, in the beginning, having escaped the influence of Henri Matisse whose sterile bouquets she would naively copy?

Let her be satisfied with visiting museums and hastily leafing through anthologies, confusing the Venetians with artists from the Ming dynasty with Ronsard and Omar-Khayyam.[218]

Miss Marthe Galard, a painter of prettiness, is an artist from the French tradition in the same vein as Mrs. Marval (though she does not have her authority) and Miss Marie Laurencin (though she does not possess her acute fantasy).[219]

---

[217] Gifted, above all, in her use of the arabesque and soft colors, Marie Laurencin (1883–1956) could not embrace the angular geometry nor the somber palette of Cubism. Her portrait of *Guillaume Apollinaire with an Egyptian Profile* of 1909–10 (Marie Laurencin Museum, Tokyo) is completely caricature. The medallions that she created for the Cubist House designed by André Mare and Raymond Duchamp-Villon in 1913 (Marie Laurencin Museum, Tokyo) were painted in an Art Deco style and have nothing to do with Cubism. [JG]

[218] To better affirm Marie Laurencin's independence, Salmon mixes up the eras, countries and the arts. Pierre de Ronsard (1524–1585), the most famous of French Renaissance poets, and the Persian poet Omar-Khayyam, who died around 1123, represent here the poetic analogy. [JG]

[219] Posterity has not remembered Marthe Galard. Apollinaire mentions her in his article "Chroniques d'art, Les Peintresses," *Le Petit Bleu*, April 5, 1912, stating, like Salmon, that she has "less authority" than Jacqueline Marval and Marie Laurencin. [JG]

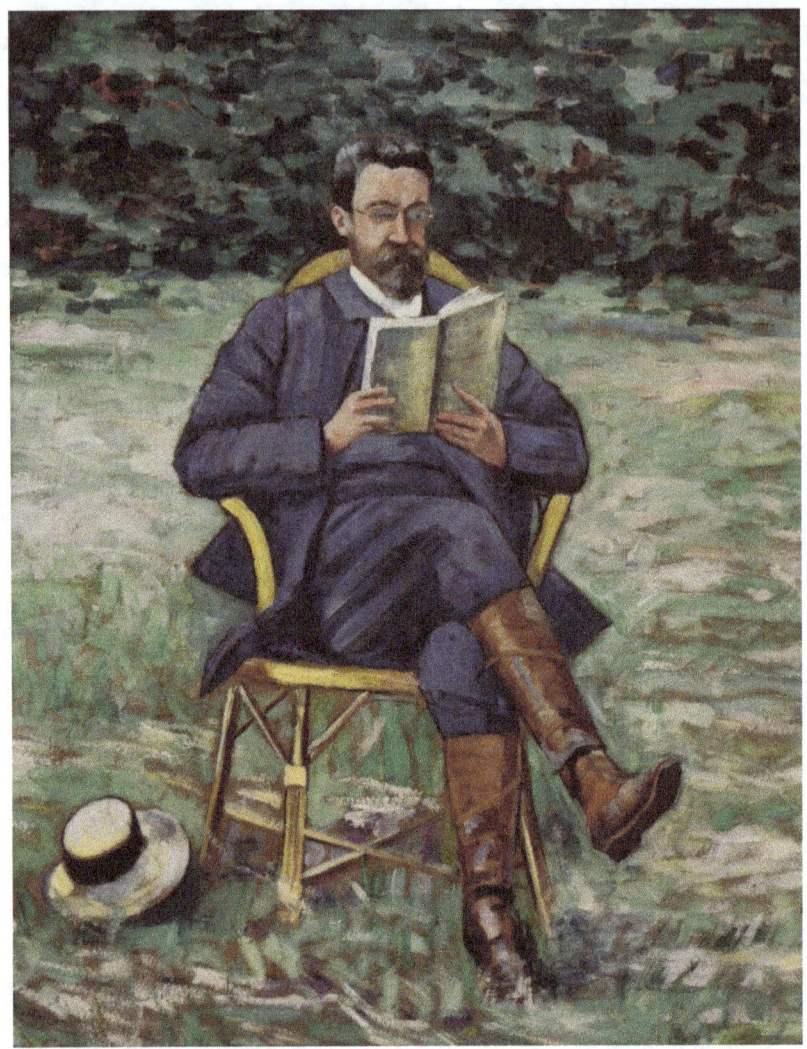

Figure 21. Georgette Agutte, *Marcel Sembat Reading*, c. 1900
Musée de Grenoble

How can we not praise the decorative abundance of Mrs. Galtier-
Boissière?[220] And could we take no further interest in the wonderful efforts of

---

[220] Louise Galtier-Boissière (1866-1957), mother of the designer and pamphleteer
Jean Galtier-Boissière (1891–1966) and the sister of the artist Émile-René Ménard (1862–
1930). [JG]

Mrs. Georgette Agutte?[221] This artist attains a severe style without consenting to the danger of emotional restraint which prevents us from fully enjoying a Vallotton,[222] to whom however she comes close. The sense of color, at the same time dazzling and limited, is not the least seductive sign of the orderly, but nevertheless picturesque, talent of Mrs. Georgette Agutte.

Nor could we neglect Misses Albertine and Suzanne Bernouard[223] whose art is minor and yet occupies a place of importance since it greatly influenced the latest women's fashions.

Misses Albertine and Suzanne Bernouard paint and embroider. It is not decorative art that led them to painting.

Knowing that applied art must reflect—and can do nothing but reflect—the latest tendencies of painting, they took up the needle without dropping the brush.

---

[221] Born in Paris, Georgette Agutte (1867–1922) came from a bourgeois background. She married the art critic and publisher Paul Flat in 1888 and through him met René Piot, a student of Gustave Moreau. She joined Moreau's studio where she met Matisse, Marquet, Camoin, Rouault and Desvallières. She divorced Flat in 1894 and three years later married the politician Marcel Sembat. Agutte exhibited in the avant-garde salons and galleries. By 1913 she created a technique for painting on fibro-cement material used in construction to produce a matte, fresco finish. Agutte committed suicide after the death of her husband on September 5, 1922. [BGN] She was one of four women included in the exhibition on avant-garde women artists *Les femmes peintres de l'avant-garde 1900–1930* (catalogue published by Somogy, Paris, 2006): Valadon, Marval, Charmy and Agutte. [JG]

[222] Félix Vallotton (1867–1925) was a Swiss painter, who has always been considered an engraver of the highest quality. His paintings, for the longest time regarded as "cold," have been rediscovered. See the catalogue for the exhibition *Félix Vallotton: Le Feu sous la glace* (*Fire under Ice*), Réunion des Musées Nationaux-Grand Palais, 2013. [JG] Also *Félix Vallotton: The Painter of Disquiet,* Metropolitan Museum of Art, New York, October 29, 2019, through January 26, 2020. [BGN]

[223] These are the sisters of François Bernouard (1884-1949), who published the album on Isadora Duncan's dances by Dunoyer de Segonzac. Albertine is not as well known as Suzanne, who married Louis Süe (1875-1968) in 1920. This architect, who was first the lover of Isadora Duncan, is considered a major figure in the Art Deco movement. In 1909 he renovated an eighteenth-century mansion for Paul Poiret at 26 rue d'Antin. It was here Picasso's *Demoiselles d'Avignon* was exhibited for the first time, in July 1916, in a show known as the "Salon d'Antin," organized by André Salmon. [JG]

They paint flowers: roses and lilies—above all roses in pinks like the faces of lovers and blues like the lunar clouds. They have imagined fabulous and lively roses, which shiver on the cushions in those drawing rooms where the most modern poems are recited and where the boldest melodies resound. One song by Ravel makes their petals shake; an elegy by Henri de Régnier brings them to life.[224] And on these cushions, adorned with harmonious reliefs, it happened that a very young poet, nonchalantly reclining, receives congratulations from a very old academician.[225]

Smitten with an art which Manzana-Pissarro[226] made known before the draftsmen of the Scheherazade school,[227] Mrs. Léone Georges-Reboux[228] imagined

---

[224] There is no need to introduce composer Maurice Ravel (1875–1937), internationally famous for his *Boléro*, music for a ballet featuring Ida Rubenstein, that premiered in 1928. In 1912, Ravel had already composed his famous *Daphnis et Chloé* for the Ballets Russes. Henri de Régnier (1864–1936) is a Post-Symbolist poet. He was elected to the Académie Française in 1911. [BGN/JG]

[225] The "very young poet" is Jean Cocteau (1889–1963), who published, at nineteen years old, *La Lampe d'Aladin* (February 1909). This first collection of poems was applauded at Anna de Noailles' salon. The "very old academician" could be the novelist Anatole France (1844–1924), who was elected to the Académie Française in 1896, and infatuated with Anna de Noailles. [JG]

[226] Georges Henri Manzana-Pissarro (1871–1961), the third child of the Impressionist Camille Pissarro, was known for his landscapes and Orientalist motifs. [BGN]

[227] A reference to the illustrators of the luxurious revue *Schéhérazade*, founded in 1909 by François Bernouard, Jean Cocteau and Maurice Rostand—the son of Edmond and the intimate friend of Marcel Proust. Contributors, among others, to the illustrations, include Albertine Bernouard, Paul Iribe, Dunoyer de Segonzac, Luc-Albert Moreau, Marie Laurencin, etc. [JG]

[228] Léone Georges (birth and death dates unknown) was married to Paul Reboux (1877–1963), a prolific writer, critic, and editor of *Le Journal*, who collaborated with his friend Charles Müller (1877–1914) on the satirical publication À la manière de. . . , which featured pastiches of well-known literary figures. [JG]

and realized for our enchantment an Orient that makes us no longer wish to know the other—the true and not the false one which is made up of consuls, reenlisted soldiers, profiteers and photographers.

Let us prefer the Orient of poets, the gallant and philosophical Orient, where Diderot knew every twist and turn,[229] and which Mrs. Léone Georges-Reboux represents with boldness and precision.

There, French actresses become dancing girls and mimes, dressed in Ispahan clothes under a Parisian hat, for some Harlequin-Pasha.[230] Too worldly to cover the world, how well acquainted Mrs. Léone Georges-Reboux is with the Asia she has not visited!

Mrs. Léone Georges-Reboux paints with the beak of a mythical Roc the thousand and one suggestive motifs of a ceiling welcoming marvelous dreams.[231]

---

[229] An allusion to a short *roman à clef* entitled *Les Bijoux indiscrets* (*The Indiscreet Jewels*), published in 1748, which tells the love affair of the Congo's Sultan Mangogul and his favorite consort Mirzoza (based on Louis XV and Madame de Pompadour). [JG]

[230] Orientalism was a fashion linked to the success of the Ballets Russes in France. On May 20, 1911, Paul Poiret invited "Tout-Paris" to his mansion on the rue d'Antin for a costume ball called "The Thousand-Second Night." The couturier was dressed as a caliph, a whip in his hand. With his favorite sultana (Mrs. Poiret), surrounded by a harem and a flock of exotic birds, they received women from highest ranks of society, actresses from the Comédie Française, and stars from the music halls. The mansion's park had been transformed into a Middle Eastern souk; monkeys and parrots were in the trees. [JG] Edwin T. Morris wrote in his book *The Scents of Time: A History of Perfume* (Metropolitan Museum of Art, 1999, 2008) that three hundred guests were invited and this may be the occasion that launched his "revolutionary design—pants for women." p. 94. [BGN]

[231] The Roc is a gigantic mythical bird found in Persian tales, such as "Sinbad the Sailor" in *A Thousand and One Nights*. [BGN]

Mrs. Elisabeth Delvolvé-Carrière evinces a filial approach that perpetuates the teaching of one of the greatest artists of the recent past, her father Eugène Carrière.[232]

Each one of her works is a homage to the memory of the master. Mrs. Elisabeth Delvolvé-Carrière, evidently a slave to the genius she did not inherit, is nevertheless an artist of talent who knew how to continue Carrière while enriching her palette with all the tones of rare and common flowers, which she loves among all that live, suffer and disappear.[233]

---

[232] Eugène Carrière (1849–1906) was a portraitist known for his smoky dark-light effects and his subtle use of grays. [JG]

[233] Note that all the women painters Salmon mentions were daughters, sisters, wives and mistresses of men who were better known at that time than themselves. Today, Marie Laurencin is still the most famous of them all—from Tokyo (where a museum is dedicated to her work) to Paris, and beyond. However, for the French, she is, above all, Guillaume Apollinaire's muse, the inspiration for his famous "Le Pont Mirabeau" in *Alcools* (1913), which the poet wrote in 1912 when their relationship ended. [JG/BGN]

POSTSCRIPT

My task is done. I have carried it out conscientiously, if not successfully.

It should be understood that, after the masters and directors, it was possible for me to cite only the leaders.

As for the Cubists, I purposely defined only their common activity. For them, the trial period for any particular body of work is still not over.

I did the most I could for the least known and the most controversial.

Those who easily triumph will agree with me and not take offense.

March–April 1912

A SELECTED BIBLIOGRAPHY

Alexander, Sidney. *Marc Chagall: A Biography*. New York: G.P. Putnam's Sons, 1978.

Anonymous. *Canadian Illustrated News*, 30 October 1869, found at the National Library of Canada website: https://www.canadiana.ca/view/oocihm.8_06230_1/7?r=0&s=1

Anonymous. *La Farce de Maître Pathelin* (c. 1465). https://www.vousnousils.fr/casden/pdf/id00100.pdf

Anonymous. *Lazarillo de Tormes (1554)* in *The Life of Lazarillo de Tormes: His Fortunes and Misfortunes as Told by Himself with a Sequel by Juan de Luna*. Translated by Robert S. Rudder and Carmen Criado. New York: Frederick Unger Publishing, 1973. (First publication in Paris, 1620.) https://www.gutenberg.org/files/53489/53489-h/53489-h.htm

Antliff, Mark, and Patricia Leighten, eds. *A Cubism Reader: Documents and Criticism*. Translations from the French by Jane Marie Todd. Chicago: University of Chicago Press, 2008.

Apollinaire, Guillaume. *Apollinaire on Art: Essays and Reviews, 1902-1918*. Edited by Leroy C. Breunig. Translated by Susan Suleiman. New York: Viking Press, 1972; New York: Da Capo Press, 1987.

Apollinaire, Guillaume. *Le Bestiaire, ou le Cortège d'Orphée*. Paris: Deplanche, 1911.

Apollinaire, Guillaume. *Méditations esthétiques: Les peintres cubists*. Paris: Eugène Figuière, 1912.

Apollinaire, Guillaume. *Oeuvres complètes de Guillaume Apollinaire*. Edited by Michel Décaudin. Paris: A. Balland and J. Lacat, 1966.

Apollinaire, Guillaume. "La Peinture Nouvelle: Notes d'art. "*Les Soirées de Paris*, April-May 1912, 113-115.

Ashton, Dore, ed. *Picasso on Art: A Selection of Views*. New York: Da Capo, 1972.

Bacou, Roseline. *Odilon Redon: Pastels.* Translated by Beatrice Rehl. New York: George Braziller, 1987.

Baldassari, Anne, Pierre Daix, Pepe Karmel, Irving Lavin, Jean-Claude Lebensztejn, and Leo Steinberg. *Cubist Picasso.* Paris: Musée National Picasso/Flammarion, 2007.

Baldassari, Anne. *Picasso and Photography: The Dark Mirror.* Translated by Deke Dusinberre. Houseton, TX: The Museum of Fine Arts/Flammarion, 1997.

Barr, Alfred H., Jr. *The Sculpture of Elie Nadelman.* Exhibition Catalogue. Museum of Modern Art, 1948.

Baudelaire, Charles. "Salon de 1846," in *Art in Paris, 1845-1862: Salons and Other Exhibitions.* Translated by Jonathan Mayne. London: Phaidon Press, 1965.

Blier, Suzanne Preston. *Picasso's Demoiselles: The Untold Origins of a Modern Masterpiece.* Durham, NC: Duke University Press, 2019.

Boime, Albert. *Art and the French Commune: Imagining Paris after War and Revolution.* Princeton, NJ: Princeton University Press, 1995.

Bois, Yve-Alain. "The Semiology of Cubism," in *Picasso and Braque: A Symposium,* edited by Lynn Zelevansky. New York: The Museum of Modern Art, 1992, 169-221.

Brauer, Fay. "Building the Body Beautiful: `La Culture Physique' and the New Artistic Anatomy in the French Radical Republic." CAA Conference, New York, February 26, 2000.

Büttner, Philippe et al. *Félix Vallotton: The Painter of Disquiet.* New York: Metropolitan Museum of Art, 2019.

Chipp, Herschel B. *Theories of Modern Art.* Berkeley: University of California, 1968.

Claudel, Paul. "Camille Claudel Statuaire." *L'Occident* (August 1905). Text reprinted in *L'Art décoratif.* July-December 1913.

Cottington, David. *Cubism.* Cambridge: Cambridge University Press, 1998.

Cottington, David. *Cubism in the Shadow of War: The Avant-Garde and Politics in Paris, 1905-1914.* New Haven, CT: Yale University Press, 1998.

Cottington, David. "What the Papers Say: Politics and Ideology in Picasso's Collages of 1912." *Art Journal* 47, no. 4 (Winter 1988): 350-359.

Cousins, Judith. "Documentary Chronology," in *Picasso and Braque: Pioneering Cubism*. Exhibition Catalogue. New York: Museum of Modern Art, 1989.

Cousins, Judith, and Hélène Seckel. "Chronology of *Les Demoiselles d'Avignon*, 1907-1939," in *Les Demoiselle d'Avignon*. New York: Museum of Modern Art, 1994, 145-205.

Daix, Pierre. *Picasso Créateur: La vie intime et l'oeuvre*. Paris: Éditions du Seuil, 1987.

Daix, Pierre. *Picasso: Life and Art*. Translated by Olivia Emmet. New York: Icon Edition/HarperCollins, 1994.

Diderot, Denis. "Salon de 1767," in *Salons*, volume III. Edited by Jean Seznec and Jean Adhémar. Oxford: Clarendon Press, 1963.

Eager, Edward. *Magic by the Lake*. San Diego: Odyssey/Harcourt, 1957, repr. 1999.

Elderfield, John. *Fauvism: The "Wild Beasts" and Its Affinities*. Exhibition Catalogue. New York: The Museum of Modern Art, 1976.

Elderfield, John. *Henri Matisse: A Retrospective*. Exhibition Catalogue. New York: Museum of Modern Art, 1992.

Elsen, Albert, and Marie Busco. *Rodin and his Contemporaries: The Iris and B. Gerald Cantor Collection*. New York: Cross River Press, 1991.

Flam, Jack. "Matisse and the Fauves," in *"Primitivism" in the 20th Century*. Exhibition Catalogue. New York: The Museum of Modern Art, 1984, 210-239.

Flandrin, Georges, and François Roussier. *Jules Flandrin, 1871-1947: un élève de Gustave Moreau témoin de son temps*. La Tronche: Éditions de l'association Flandrin Deloras, 1992.

Flaubert, Gustave. *Bouvard and Pécuchet*. Translated by T.W. Earp and G.W. Stonier. New York: New Directions, 1954.

Flaubert, Gustave. *Madame Bovary* (1857). Translated by Geoffrey Wall. London: Penguin Classics, 2003.

France, Anatole (pseudonym of Jacques-Anatole-François Thibaut). *The Amethyst Ring* (*L'Anneau d'améthyste*, 1899). Translated by B. Drillien. New York: Dodd, Mead and Company, 1923.

France, Anatole. *The Elm-Tree on the Mall* (*L'Orme du mail*, 1897). Translated by M.P. Willcocks. New York: Dodd, Mead, 1926.

France, Anatole. *Golden Tales of Anatole France*. New York: Dodd, Mead, 1926.

France, Anatole. *Monsieur Bergeret in Paris* (*M. Bergeret à Paris*, 1901). Translated by B. Drillien. London: John Lane, 1922.

France, Anatole. *The Wicker-Wood Woman* (*Le Mannequin d'osier*, 1897). Translated by M.P. Willcocks. New York: Dodd, Mead, 1922.

Fusco, Peter and H.W. Janson, eds. *The Romantics to Rodin*. Exhibition Catalogue. Los Angeles: Los Angeles County Museum, 1980.

Gauguin, Paul. *The Writings of a Savage*, edited by Daniel Guérin and translated by Eléonor Levieux. New York: Viking Press, 1974.

Gedo, Mary Mathews. *Picasso: Art as Autobiography*. Chicago: University of Chicago Press, 1980.

Gersh-Nešić, Beth S. "André Salmon, Pablo Picasso and the History of Cubism," *André Salmon, poète de l'Art vivant,* in the series *Var et Poésie,* no. 8. Michèle Monte and Jacqueline Gojard, eds. Toulon-Var: Université du Sud, 2010: 295-308.https://babel.univ-tln.fr/vp-07-andre-salmon-poete-de-lart-vivant/

Gersh-Nešić, Beth S. "Cézannisme and Cézannismes: Examining the Literature on Cubism." Mediterranean Studies Conference, Aix-en-Provence, May 2001.

Gersh-Nešić, Beth S. "Countertransference and Critical Discourse: The Case of André Salmon and Guillaume Apollinaire," *Art Criticism*, v. 7, no. 2 (1992): 79-88.

Gersh-Nešić, Beth S. "An Anecdotal History of *Les Demoiselles d'Avignon*" and "*Les Demoiselles d'Avignon* Revisited: Appreciation and Appropriation," in the exhibition catalogue *The Demoiselles Revisited*. New York: Francis Naumann Fine Art, 2007.

Gersh-Nešić, Beth S. *The Early Criticism of André Salmon: A Study of His Thoughts of Cubism.* New York: Garland Publishing, 1991.

Gersh-Nešić, Beth S. "From Paris to New York: The Life of the *Demoiselles*," in the exhibition catalogue *Staring Back: On Picasso's "Demoiselles d'Avignon."* Burlington, VT: The Fleming Museum/University of Vermont, 2015, 16-23.

Gersh-Nešić, Beth S. "The Marvelous Madame Marval: A Woman Artist Among the Fauves." *Bonjour Paris*, April 7, 2020. https://bonjourparis.com/history/the-marvelous-madame-marval-a-woman-artist-among-the-fauves/

Gilot, Françoise. *Matisse and Picasso: A Friendship in Art.* New York: Doubleday, 1990.

Gleizes, Albert, and Jean Metzinger. *Du Cubism.* Paris: Eugène Figuière, 1912.

Gojard, Jacqueline. "Au rendez-vous des poètes," in the exhibition catalogue *L'École de Paris, 1904-1923, La Part de l'autre.* Paris: Musée d'art moderne de la Ville de Paris, 2000.

Gojard, Jacqueline. "Carte blanche à André Salmon." Radio-Marseille, 12 November 1992.

Gojard, Jacqueline. "Étude du `Manucript Trouvé dans un Chapeau' d'André Salmon," unpublished dissertation for the Université de Paris-Sorbonne, Littérature Française, 1985.

Gojard, Jacqueline. "Le Nominalism d'André Salmon," in *André Salmon: Quaderni del Novecento Francese* 9, edited by P.A. Jannini and S. Zappi (Rome: Bulzoni; Paris: Nizet, 1987), 49-73.

Gojard, Jacqueline. "L'œuvre d'André Salmon ou la fable de l'Art vivant, " in *André Salmon, poète de l'Art vivant*, in the series *Var et Poésie*, no 8. Michèle Monte and Jacqueline Gojard, eds. Toulon-Var: Université du Sud, 2010: 25-38. https://babel.univ-tln.fr/vp-07-andre-salmon-poete-de-lart-vivant/

Gojard, Jacqueline. *Pablo Picasso and André Salmon: The Painter, the Poet and the Portraits.* New York: Za Mir Press, 2019.

Gojard, Jacqueline. "'Ut pictura poësis' tentative de restitution d'un art poétique, à partir de *Peindre* d'André Salmon," in *Définitions et redéfinitions de la poésie française (1900-1939)*. Warsaw: University of Warsaw, 1999: 69-82.

Goncourt, Edmond de, and Jules de Goncourt. *Manette Salomon* (1867). Paris: L'Harmattan, 1993.

Gourmont, Rémy de. "Celui qui ne comprend pas," in *Essais d'Art Libre*, no. 7 (August 1892).

Gourmont, Rémy de. "L'Idealisme," in *Le Chemin de Velours*. Paris: Mercure de France, 1902.

Green, Christopher. *Art in France, 1910-1940*. New Haven, CT: Yale University Press, 2000.

Green, Christopher. *Cubism and Its Enemies*. New Haven, CT: Yale University Press, 1987.

Henderson, Linda Dalrymple. *The Fourth Dimension and Non-Euclidean Geometry in Modern Art*. Princeton, NJ: Princeton University Press, 1983.

Hourcade, Olivier. "La Tendance de la peinture contemporaine (notes pour une causerie sur l'art contemporain)." *Revue de France et des Pays français*, February 1912, 35-41.

Humphrey, Richard. *Futurism*. Cambridge: Cambridge University Press, 1999.

Hutton, John G. *Neo-Impressionism and the Search for Solid Ground: Art, Science, and Anarchism in Fin-de-Siècle France*. Baton Rouge: Louisiana State University Press, 1994.

Kangaslahti, Kate. "École de Paris: Inside and Out: Reconsidering the Experience of the Foreign Artist in Interwar France." *Crossing Cultures: Conflict, Migration and Convergence, The Proceedings of the 32nd International Congress of the History of Art*. Melbourne: The Miegunyah Press, 2009: 602-66.

Kangaslahti, Kate. "Foreign Artists and the École de Paris: Critical and Institutional Ambivalence Between the Wars." *Academics, Pompiers, Official Artists and the Arrière-garde: Defining Modern and Traditional in France, 1900-1960*. Natalie Adamson and Toby Norris, editors. Newcastle upon Tyne: Cambridge Scholars Publishing, 2009: 85-111.

Karmel, Pepe. *Picasso and the Invention of Cubism*. New Haven, CT: Yale University Press, 2003.

Kirstein, Lincoln. *Elie Nadelman.* New York: The Eakins Press, 1973.

Krauss, Rosalind. "Motivation of the Sign," in *Picasso and Braque: A Symposium.* New York: Museum of Modern Art, 1992, 261-286.

Lee, Jane. *Derain.* New York: Universe/Oxford: Phaidon, 1990.

Leighten, Patricia, and Mark Antliff, eds. *A Cubism Reader: Documents and Criticism.* Translations from the French by Jane Marie Todd. Chicago: University of Chicago Press, 2008.

Leighten, Patricia. "Picasso's Collages and the Threat of War, 1912-13," *Art Bulletin* 67, no. 4 (December 1985): 653-672.

Leighten, Patricia. *Re-Ordering the Universe: Picasso and Anarchism, 1897-1914.* Princeton, NJ: Princeton University Press, 1989.

Leighten, Patricia. "The White Peril and L'Art Nègre: Picasso, Primitivism, and Anticolonialism." *Art Bulletin* vol. 72, no. 4 (December 1990): 609-630.

Margerie, Laure de. *"La Danse" de Carpeaux.* Paris: Éditions de la Réunion des musées nationaux, 1989.

Markus, Ruth. "Picasso's Guitar, 1912: The Transition from Analytical to Synthetic Cubism," in *Assaph: Studies in Art History* 2 (Tel Aviv: Tel Aviv University--The Yolanda and David Katz Faculty of Art, 1996): 233-246.

Matisse, Henri. "Matisse Speaks," statements to E. Teriade, *Art News Annual,* 21. New York: Simon and Shuster, 1952, 40-77.

Marval, Jacqueline: https://www.jacqueline-marval.com/

Metzinger, Jean. "Cubisme et Tradition," *Paris Journal,* 16 August 1911.

Metzinger, Jean. "Note sur la peinture," *Pan,* October-November 1910, 649-51.

Mirbeau, Octave. *Sébastien Roch.* Translated by Nicoletta Simborowski. Cambridge: Dedalus, 2000.

Monte, Michèle, ed., with the collaboration of Jacqueline Gojard. *André Salmon, poète de l'Art vivant,* in the series *Var et Poésie,* no 8. Toulon-Var: Université du Sud, 2010.

Morice, Charles. "Salon des Indépendants," *Mercure de France,* 16 April 1909.

Musée de Pont-Aven. *Maurice Asselin et la Bretagne*. Pont-Aven: Musée des Beaux-Arts de Pont-Aven, 2002.

Nietzsche, Friedrich. *Thus Spake Zarathustra*, in *The Portable Nietzsche*. Translated by Walter Kaufman. New York: Viking Press, 1954, repr. 1968.

Nerval, Gérard de. *Sylvie: Souvenir du Valois* (1853), in *Oeuvres complètes, volume I*. Paris: Gallimard, 1966, 241-273.

Olivier, Fernande. *Picasso and his Friends*, translated by Jane Miller. New York: Appleton-Century, 1965.

Olivier, Fernande. *Picasso et ses amis*. Paris: Librarie Stock, 1933.

Paret, Michèle. "Biographie," in *Albert Marquet, du fauvisme à l'impressionnisme*. Exhibition Catalogue. Paris: Musée national d'art moderne, Centre Pompidou/Troyes: Musée d'Art moderne de Troyes, 2003, 99-127.

Paris, Reine-Marie. *Camille*. Paris: Gallimard, 1984; Translated by Liliane Emery Tuck. New York: Seaver Books, 1988.

Paul, Barbara. *Hugo de Tschudi und die Moderne französische Kunst in Deutschen Kaiserrich*. Mainz: P. von Zabern, 1993.

Perry, Gillian. *Women Artists and the Parisian Avant-Garde*. New York: St. Martin's Press, 1995.

Picasso, Pablo, to Marius De Zayas, "Picasso Speaks." *The Arts* v. 3 (May 1923): 315-326.

Poe, Edgar Allan. "Man of the Crowd" (1840) in *Great Tales and Poems of Edgar Allan Poe*. New York: Pocket Books/Washington Square Press, 1951.

Poggi, Christine. *In Defiance of Painting: Cubism, Futurism, and the Invention of Collage*. New Haven, CT: Yale University Press, 1992.

Puy, Michel. "Le Dernier État de la peinture," *Mercure de France*, 16 July 1910, 243-266; as a book Paris : Union française d'édition, 1911.

Puy, Michel. *L'Effort des peintres moderne*s. Paris: Albert Messein, 1933.

Puy, Michel. "Les Indépendants." *Les Marges*, July 1911, 27-30.

Renard, Jules. *Poil de Carotte; avec 50 dessins de F. Vallotton*. Paris: E. Flammarion, 1894.

Reward, John. *Post-Impressionism: From van Gogh to Gauguin*. New York: Museum of Modern Art/Boston: New York Graphic Society, 3rd ed., 1978.

Richardson, John, with Marilyn McCully. *A Life of Picasso, volume I: 1881-1906*. New York: Random House, 1991.

Richardson, John, with Marilyn McCully. *A Life of Picasso, volume II: 1907-1917*. New York: Random House, 1996.

Rimbaud, Arthur. *Complete Works*. Translated by Paul Schmidt. New York: Harper and Row, 1975.

Rivière, Jacques. "Sur les tendances actuelles de la peinture." *Revue d'Europe et d'Amerique*, March 1, 1912, 384-406.

Robbins, Daniel. *Jean Metzinger in Retrospect*. Exhibition Catalogue. Iowa City: University of Iowa Museum of Art, 1985.

Roos, Jane Mayo. *Early Impressionism and the French State (1866-1874)*. Cambridge: Cambridge University Press, 1996.

Rose, June. *Modigliani: The Pure Bohemian*. New York: St. Martin's Press, 1990.

Rosenblum, Robert. "Picasso and the Typography of Cubism," in *Picasso in Retrospect*, edited by Roland Penrose and John Golding (New York: Harper and Row, 1973; Icon Editions, 1980): 33-47.

Rousseau, Eloi. *Un Fauve Chez Bonnard: Henri Manguin et l'exaltation de la couleur*. Milan: Silvana Editore/Musée Bonnard, 2015.

Roussier, François, and Georges Flandrin. *Jules Flandrin, 1871-1947: un élève de Gustave Moreau témoin de son temps*. La Tronche: Éditions de l'association Flandrin Deloras, 1992.

Roussier, François. *Jacqueline Marval, 1866-1932*. Grenoble: Édition Didier Richard, 1987.

Roussier, François. *Jacqueline Marval, 1866-1932*. Paris: Édition Thalia, 2008.

Royère, Jean. "*Le Calumet*," *La Phalange*, no. 51 (20 September 1910): 8.

Rubin, William. "Cézannisme and the Beginnings of Cubism," in *Cézanne: The Late Work*. Exhibition Catalogue. New York: The Museum of Modern Art, 1977, 151-202.

Rubin, William. "The Genesis of *Les Demoiselle d'Avignon*," in *Les Demoiselles d'Avignon* [New York: The Museum of Modern Art, 1994], 13-144; originally "La Génese des *Demoiselles d'Avignon*," in *"Les Demoiselles d'Avignon."* Exhibition Catalogue. Paris: Musée Picasso, 1988, 367-489.

Rubin, William with Judith Cousins, *Picasso and Braque: Pioneering Cubism.* Exhibition Catalogue. New York: The Museum of Modern Art, 1989.

Salmon, André. *L'Art vivant.* Paris: Editions G. Crès et Cie., 1920.

Salmon, André. (La Palette). "Courriers des ateliers." *Paris-Journal,* 11 January 1912, 4.

Salmon, André. (La Palette). "Courriers des ateliers." *Gil Blas,* 1 November 1912, 4.

Salmon, André. "Carnet de Paris et d'ailleurs," *Revue littéraire de Paris et de Champagne,* no. 32 (November) and no. 33 (December).

Salmon, André. *La jeune peinture française.* Paris: Albert Messein, 1912.

Salmon, André. *La jeune sculpture française.* Paris: Albert Messein, 1919.

Salmon, André. *Le Manuscrit trouvé dans un chapeau* (1905-1919), edited and with an introduction by Jacqueline Gojard. Paris: Fata Morgana, 1983.

Salmon, André. *Le Manuscrit trouvé dans un chapeau (1905-1919).* Paris: Société littéraire de France, 1919; Libraire Stock, 1924.

Salmon, André. "Mouvement des idées: Origines et intentions du cubisme." *Demain* 68 (26 April 1919): 485-489.

Salmon, André. "Observations Déplacées." *Les Soirées de Paris,* no. 1 (February 1912): 28-30.

Salmon, André. (La Palette). Pataphysique in "Courriers des ateliers." *Paris-Journal,* 1 December 1911.

Salmon, André. *Peindre.* Paris: La Sirène, 1919.

Salmon, André. *Prikaz.* Paris: La Sirène, 1919.

Salmon, André. *Propos d'Atelier.* Paris: G. Crès, 1922.

Salmon, André. *Saint André.* Paris: Gallimard, 1936.

Salmon, André. *Souvenirs sans fin: L'air de la Butte.* Paris: La Nouvelle France, 1945. Reprinted as: *L'air de la Butte.* Paris: Arcadia, 2003.

Salmon, André. *Souvenirs sans fin, Première Époque (1903-1908)*. Paris: Gallimard, 1955; Paris: Gallimard, 2004.

Salmon, André. *Souvenirs sans fin, Deuxième Époque II (1908-1920)*. Paris: Gallimard, 1956; Paris: Gallimard, 2004.

Silver, Kenneth. *The Circle of Montparnasse: Jewish Artists in Paris, 1905-1945.* Exhibition Catalogue New York: The Jewish Museum, 1985.

Simpson, Juliet. *Jules Flandrin (1871-1947): The Other Fin de Siècle.* Oxford: Ashmolean Museum/Buckinghamshire Chilterns University College, 2001.

Stein, Gertrude. *The Autobiography of Alice B. Toklas.* New York: Vintage Books, 1933, repr. 1961.

Stolkin, Jenifer. "The Poetry of André Salmon." Master's thesis, St. Hughes College, Oxford University, 1970.

Tabarant, Adolphe. "Impressions quotidiennes." *La Petite République*, 16 December 1894, 1.

Uhde, Wilhelm. *Henri Rousseau*. Paris, Falguière, 1911.

Vauxcelles, Louis. "Exposition Braque. Chez Kahnweiler, 28 rue Vignon." *Gil Blas*, 14 November 1908.

Vauxcelles, Louis. Review of *La jeune peinture française*, "Courriers des Ateliers." *Gil Blas*, 21 October 1912.

Villiers de l'Isle Adam, Jean-Marie-Mathias-Philippe-Auguste, comte de. *Tribulat Bonhomet* (1887). Paris: J. Corti, 1967.

Wagner, Anne Middleton. *Jean-Baptiste Carpeaux: Sculptor of the Second Empire*. New Haven, CT: Yale University Press, 1986.

Ward, Martha. "From Art Criticism to Art News: Journalistic Reviewing in Late-Nineteeth-Century Paris," in *Art Criticism and its Institutions in Nineteenth-Century France*, edited by Michael R. Orwicz (Manchester: Manchester University Press, 1994), 162-181.

Weiss, Jeffrey. *The Popular Culture of Modern Art: Picasso, Duchamp, and Avant-Gardism*. New Haven, CT: Yale University Press, 1994.

Wilkin, Karen. *Braque*. New York: Abbeville, 1991.

ANDRÉ SALMON (1881-1969)

P oet, art critic, novelist, journalist, playwright, and memoirist, André Salmon was a jack of all literary trades: poet, art critic, journalist, novelist, playwright, song writer, chronicler, and memoirist. He was also a curator and active member of several artistic circles – most notably Picasso's Gang and Paul Fort's *Vers et Prose* literary tribe.

He was a much beloved storyteller, advocate for the avant-garde and an influential leader among literary and art giants.

Born in Paris on October 4, 1881 into a Leftist environment, he lived in St. Petersburg, Russia from 1897 to 1902 (first with his family while his sculptor-engraver father completed a commission and then on his own). During this formative period, he worked for the French Consulate. This influential period of his life predisposed Salmon toward friendships with artists from Russia and Eastern Europe who moved to Paris. It also inspired the erroneous factoid, oft repeated, that Salmon was a Russian Jew. He was neither.

After returning to France to complete his military service (he was quickly dismissed because of his weak constitution), Salmon embarked on a career as a poet, discovered the *La Plume* crowd, and met Guillaume Apollinaire. He has been identified as part of the Post-Symbolist Movement.

In 1904, he met Pablo Picasso and Max Jacob in Montmartre. Along with Guillaume Apollinaire, this foursome became the core of *la bande à Picasso*.

As the other *bande* members created the first major works before World War I, Salmon attained an influential position in avant-garde circles. After World War I, Picasso, Max Jacob and Apollinaire caught up with him and eventually eclipsed him.

Following World War I, Salmon continued to write prose, poetry, and art criticism, adding journalism for more income. He covered trials, crimes, and wars, including the Spanish Civil War. Sent on assignment by *Le Petit Parsien*, Salmon agreed to cover the Francoist perspective as a journalist, not a sympathizer. Picasso was incensed and refused to communicate with Salmon until 1951, when they reconciled.

From the 1920s through the invasion of France by the Nazis, Salmon wrote articles for *Le Petit Parisien*. Upon his return, he found the newspaper under Vichy control. Penniless, he had to accept their offer to write art criticism. To his mind, a nonpartisan position. After a period of censure for working for this Vichy government newspaper, Salmon was exonerated. In 1961, Salmon took up permanent residence in his summer home in the South of France (Sanary), where he ran for office in 1963. In 1964, he received the Grand Prix for poetry from the French Academy, and in 1967, Salmon became a Commander of the Order of Arts and Letters.

Salmon married twice: Jeanne Blazy-Escarpette in 1909 (who died in 1949) and Léo (Angèle Myey) in 1953. He died in Sanary, on March 12, 1969.

As an art critic, Salmon wrote about Picasso's studio activities and innovations with unwavering support at every stage. In his first book on contemporary French art, in which he coined the term "young French painting," Salmon introduced Cubism to his readers by way of an "anecdotal history." The book was written during the spring of 1912, just as this revolutionary movement gained traction within the avant-garde art world. Meanwhile, it shocked and dismayed almost everyone else. Here too in this slim volume, Salmon contextualized Cubism among the other avant-garde movements, including Fauvism and various "independents" whose painting Salmon calls "Living Art," another coined term that signified fertile contemporary directions. *La Jeune Peinture Française* (*Young French Painting*) remains a valuable source for art history scholars because of its second chapter on Cubism, where Salmon positions Picasso's shocking *Les Demoiselles d'Avignon* (1907) at the foundation of Cubism. Renowned Salmon scholar Jacqueline Gojard, Ph.D., provides an introduction to Salmon book so that readers can appreciate its daring selections of promising emerging artists including Picasso's *Demoiselles*, still unknown to the public in 1912. In July 1916, Salmon's brought Picasso's giant canvas out of the studio and into its first exhibition, "Modern Art in France," the Salon d'Antin. In *Pablo Picasso, André Salmon and "Young French Painting"* we include the only other public access to *Les Demoiselles d'Avignon*, a photograph published in the American magazine *Architectural Record*, May 1910.

Young French Painting, written in 1912, paints a true picture of the competitive French artworld between 1905 and April 1912, when he finished the book. In October 1912, *Young French Painting* hit the bookstores, just as the historic exhibitions *The Golden Section* and Salon d'Automne, which featured Cubism, opened to the public. In December 1912, Albert Gleizes and Jean Metzinger published *On Cubism* and in 1913, Guillaume Apollinaire published *The Cubist Painters: Aesthetic Meditations.*

Two years later, before World War I, Salmon completed the pendant book *La Jeune Sculpture française* (*Young French Sculpture*), wherein we learn of Picasso and Braque's artistic personalities and Picasso's astonishing new invention: the construction known as *Guitar* (both versions belong to the Museum of Modern Art in New York). *Young French Sculpture* was published in 1919.

ABOUT THE AUTHOR

of Introduction and Co-Translator

Jacqueline Gojard, Ph.D., maître de conférences hors classe, Department of Literature, University of Paris 3, Sorbonne nouvelle, has published numerous books and essays on Salmon and other French literary figures as well as edited Salmon's novels, memoirs, chronicles, a bibliography of his work and letters to/from Max Jacob (Gallimard, 2009) and Guillaume Apollinaire (Claire Paulhan, April 2022). She edited in the facsimile version of Salmon's masterpiece *Le Manuscrit trouvé dans un chapeau chapeau* [*The Manuscript Found in a Hat*] (Fata Morgana, 1983), with drawings by Picasso (originally published by La Société littéraire de France, 1919). Her doctoral dissertation (Paris Sorbonne, 1985) is a study of this work. She prefaced the new edition of *La Négresse du Sacré-Cœur* (Gallimard 2009), followed by Salmon's unpublished text "Véritable clé d'un domaine imaginaire" ["The Real Key to an Imaginary Domaine"]. Léo Salmon asked her to be the executor of André Salmon's literary estate.

ABOUT THE EDITOR

and Co-Translator

B eth S. Gersh-Nešić, Ph.D., is an art historian and the director of the New York Arts Exchange. Her work on André Salmon includes *The Early Criticism of André Salmon: A Study of His Thoughts on Cubism* (Garland Publishing, 1991); *André Salmon on French Modern Art* (Cambridge University Press, 2005), her translation and annotation of Salmon's *La Jeune Peinture française* and *La Jeune Sculpture française*; *The Demoiselles Revisited* (Francis Naumann Fine Art, 2007); and "The Anecdotal History of *Les Demoiselles d'Avignon*," for the exhibition catalogue *Staring Back: The Creation and Legacy of Picasso's "Demoiselles d'Avignon"* (Burlington, VT: Fleming Museum, February-June 2015).

Professor Gojard and Dr. Gersh-Nešić published their translation of "From Plaisance to Opéra," a chapter in Salmon's *L'Air de la Butte*, in **A***TA Source: The Online Publication of Its Literary Division* (no. 51, Spring 2011): 20-27.

INDEX

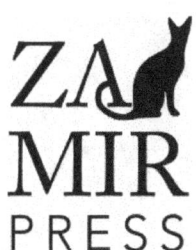

ZA MIR PRESS

A division of

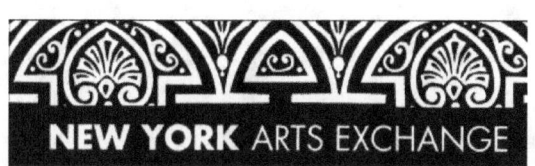

NEW YORK ARTS EXCHANGE

www.nyarts-exchange.com
www.andresalmon.org

www.ingramcontent.com/pod-product-compliance
Lightning Source LLC
Chambersburg PA
CBHW081559220526
45468CB00010B/2693